W9-BLS-053

ALSO BY ANNIE PROULX

March 6 '05

Nice day. Drove over to Bird Cloud. Spent hours looking at everything on south side.

There was one visible TA cow on north shore. Must have
 a) broke through fence somewhere
 b) climbed down into ditch (dry at this time of year) and up the other side.
 c) somebody left TA gate open?
How do we solve this problem? Put something in ditch for necessary period + remove when water comes?

First thing that met my horrified eyes was the spruce tree Daryl James planted at entrance — utterly stripped. About 8 trees and shrubs damaged by porcupine(s). Called Daryl J. but he was in Denver. His mother said "porcupines are very agile." Next day Daryl called after examining the damage. He says they are forcing in under the fence and that the damage all looks recent. He + Dave will pay a visit at dusk and see if they can get the banqueters. He suggested I get my porcupine recipes ready. I thought Ashbury-Sater did have porcupine recipes — a game cook book that recommends skunk, woodchuck + crow is pretty all-embracing — but they gave NO porcupine recipes. They did briefly detail Indian way of dealing with porcupines: (Presumably gut first? Or after singeing?)

 1. Remove useful quills for grillwork
 2. Singe off hair
 3. Prepare favorite style

and did I see a prairie dog on Olsen's side of fence on lower section?

Saw many birds: 5 bald eagles flying off west end of cliff
                 2 goldens   "   " east " "   "
                 1 harrier cruising Olsen's strip

 In water: many Canada geese, 10 mallards, 6-8 buffleheads, 3 mergansers, and, at east end between my line + Foote fishing access 2 common loons. A big golden eagle glided into a tree not far from the loons and sat waiting for one of them (perhaps) to swim under the tree and be nabbed.

Walking back I could see up where island channel mouth opens to river two bald eagles standing on gravel bar? in the river up to their ankles, obviously fishing.

BIRD CLOUD

A MEMOIR

ANNIE PROULX

SCRIBNER

New York   London   Toronto   Sydney

SCRIBNER
A Division of Simon & Schuster, Inc.
1230 Avenue of the Americas
New York, NY 10020

First Scribner hardcover edition January 2011

SCRIBNER and design are registered trademarks of The Gale Group, Inc.,
used under license by Simon & Schuster, Inc., the publisher of this work.

For information about special discounts for bulk purchases,
please contact Simon & Schuster Special Sales at 1-866-506-1949
or business@simonandschuster.com.

The Simon & Schuster Speakers Bureau can bring authors to your live event.
For more information or to book an event contact the Simon & Schuster Speakers
Bureau at 1-866-248-3049 or visit our website at www.simonspeakers.com.

DESIGNED BY ERICH HOBBING

Manufactured in the United States of America

1   3   5   7   9   10   8   6   4   2

Library of Congress Cataloging-in-Publication Data is available

ISBN 978-0-7432-8880-4
ISBN 978-1-4391-7171-4 (ebook)

1-3-11

For Harry Teague who designed it
and for the James Gang who built it
and for Dudley Gardner who dug it

. . . a very curious dish of Viennese sausages which were sizzling hot at one end and frozen at the other— a striking example of the non-conductivity of sausages in high altitudes.

—H. W. Tilman

Contents

BIRD CLOUD

The Back Road
to Bird Cloud

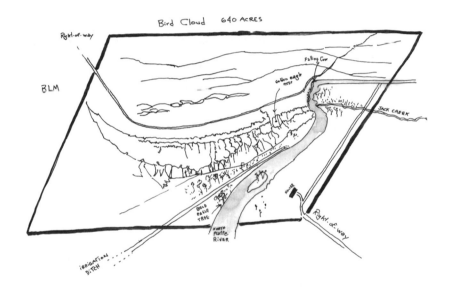

March 2005

The cow-speckled landscape is an ashy grey color. I am driving through flat pastureland on a rough county road that is mostly dirt, the protective gravel long ago squirted into ditches by speeding ranch trucks. Stiffened tire tracks veer off the road, through mud and into the sagebrush, the marks of someone

1

with back pasture business. It is too early for grass and the ranchers are still putting out hay, the occasional line of tumbled green alfalfa the only color in a drab world. The cows are strung out in a line determined by the rancher's course across the field; their heads are down and they pull at the bright hay.

The blue-white road twists like an overturned snake showing its belly. The ditches alongside are the same grey noncolor as the dust that coats the sage and rabbitbrush, the banks sloping crumbles of powdery soil that say "not far away from here were once volcanoes." It is impossible not to think about those old ash-spewing volcanoes when moving through Wyoming. The sagebrush seems nearly black and beaten low by the ceaseless wind. Why would anybody live here, I think. I live here.

But it is a different world down by the river at Bird Cloud. On the north bank rears a four-hundred-foot cliff, the creamy caprock a crust of ancient coral. This monolith has been tempered by thousands of years of polishing wind, blowtorch sun, flood and rattling hail, sluice of rain. After rain the cliff looks bruised, dark splotches and vertical channels like old scars. Two miles west the cliff shrinks into ziggurat stairs of dark, iron-colored stone. At the east end of the property the cliff shows a fault, a diagonal scar that a geologist friend says is likely related to the Rio Grande Rift which is slowly tearing the North American continent apart. In no place that I've ever lived have I thought so often about the subterranean movements of continents. The fault in the cliff is a reminder that the earth is in slow, constant flux, inexorably shoving continental plates together, pulling them apart, making new oceans and enormous supercontinents, a vast new Pangaea Proxima predicted hundreds of millions of years from now, long after our species has exited the scene. The Rio Grande Rift deformation, which started 30 million years ago in the Cenozoic, is a stretching and thinning of the earth's crust by upward-bulging forces in the churning heat of the mantle deep below. The rift extends from West Texas and New Mexico to about twenty miles north of Bird Cloud, and has made not only the Rio Grande River gorge near Taos but some of the west's most beautiful valleys.[1] In fact the rift seems to be related to western basin and range topography. The diagonal fault in Bird Cloud's cliff as well as the cliff's entire sloping shape and the existence of Jack Creek, a feeder stream, are all likely influenced by this irresistible stretching force.

Another way I think about Bird Cloud's golden cliff is to remember Uluru in Australia's red center. Thomas Keneally wrote rhapsodically of the rock's "sublime sandstone conglomerate" which evenly spalls its outer layers so that its profile never changes although it becomes incrementally smaller as the centuries pass.[2] This massive megalith, not far from Alice Springs, I saw in 1996 with artist Claire Van Vliet who was sketching nearby Kata Tjuta—rock formations that resemble huge stone turbans.

The resemblances of the Bird Cloud property to Uluru are several, though perhaps a little far-fetched. The two sites are roughly the same size and bulk and go through color shifts according to time of day. Both seem to be fitted with interior lights that create a glow after dark. Uluru has its pools and twisting watercourses down the huge body of the rock; the cliff has the river at its foot. Both Uluru and Kata Tjuta are extremely important in matters spiritual and ceremonial to Aboriginal tribes, especially the Pitjantjatjara and Yankunt-jatjara western desert tribes, but the story of how the Tradi-

---

1. Most of the older sources place the northernmost snout of the Rio Grande Rift in Colorado, but recent work from University of Wyoming geologists places it in south-central Wyoming.

2. Thomas Keneally, *Outback* (Sydney: Hodder and Stoughton, 1983), 19.

tional Owners lost these places to the federal government is familiar, sad and ugly. In the 1985 "agreement" between the Anangu, the Aboriginal people of the area, and the government, the Anangu were forced to lease Uluru and Kata Tjuta to the National Park Service and to allow tourists to climb Uluru. Despite the unenforceable rule on a Park Service sign stating that the Traditional Owners regard climbing the rock as a desecration, thousands insultingly climb it every year. In my part of Wyoming, Bird Cloud's cliffs were once a much-used camping place for western Indian tribes, the Ute, Arapaho, Shoshone, maybe Sioux and Cheyenne. Nearby Elk Mountain was a place marker indicating a mutually agreed on battleground area.

The geography around Uluru is laced with ancient hero trails that have existed since the Dreamtime. It is a place of ritual caves where certain important ceremonies of the world's most ancient culture still take place, where there are sacred fertility stones known to few living mortals and pools where legendary events occurred. Following the infrequent rains, twisting streams of water flow down the red flanks and into various pools. At Uluru the general slope of the great rock is reversed by a fold called Kandju, according to Keneally, "a benevolent lizard who came to Ayers Rock to find his boomerang."[3] And Bird Cloud's yellow cliff tapers away at its east end and is balanced by the distant rise of Pennock, a reverse image of slope.

Along Jack Creek the leafless willow stems burn red as embers. Willow is cautious, one of the last shrubs to put out its leaves—there is frost danger until mid-June. The cliff is reflected in the onyx river, and swimming across it is the stout beaver with a bank den on the far side. The beaver disappears into the brilliant *Salix* stems.

3. Keneally, *Outback,* 19.

This place is, perhaps, where I will end my days. Or so I think.

Well do I know my own character negatives—bossy, impatient, reclusively shy, short-tempered, single-minded. The good parts are harder to see, but I suppose a fair dose of sympathy and even compassion is there, a by-product of the writer's imagination. I can and do put myself in others' shoes constantly. Observational skills, quick decisions (not a few bad ones), and a tendency to overreach, to stretch comprehension and try difficult things are part of who I am. History seized me a long time ago. I am like Luigi Pirandello's character Dr. Fileno,

> who thought he had found an efficacious remedy for all human ills, an infallible recipe capable of bringing solace to himself and all mankind in case of any calamity whatever, public or private.
>
> Actually it was more than a remedy or a recipe that Doctor Fileno had discovered; it was a method consisting in reading history books from morning till night and practicing looking at the present as though it were an event already buried in the archives of the past. By this method he had cured himself of all suffering and of all worry, and without having to die had found a stern, serene peace, imbued with that particular sadness which cemeteries would still preserve even if all men on earth were dead. [4]

That attitude may have something to do with building a house suited to one's interests, needs and character. Basically I

4. Luigi Pirandello, "La tragedia d'un personaggio" [A Character's Tragedy], in *Eleven Short Stories,* trans. Stanley Appelbaum (New York: Dover, 1994), 149.

live alone, although summers are a constant stream of visitors and friends. I need room for thousands of books and big worktables where I can heap manuscripts, research material, where I can spread out maps. Books are very important to me. I wish I could think of them as some publishers do—as "product"—but I can't. I have lived in many houses, most inadequate and chopped into awkward spaces, none with enough book space. When I was a child we moved oftcn, sometimes every year. My father worked in New England's textile mills, trying hard to overcome his French Canadian background by switching jobs, always moving up the various ladders of his ambition: "bigger and better jobs and more money," he said.

The first house I can remember vividly was a tiny place in northeastern Connecticut, not far from Willimantic, a house which my parents rented during the late 1930s from a Polish family named Wozniak. I liked that name, Wozniak. I can draw that house from memory although I was two to three years old when we lived there.

I have a keen memory of dizziness as I tried to climb the stairs, of being held fast when my sweater snagged on a nail. I was coming down with some illness, the dizzy sensation and the relentless nail still vivid after seventy years. When I was sick I was moved from my bed upstairs to a cot by the kitchen window. My mother gave me a box of Chiclets chewing gum, the first I had ever seen. One by one I licked the smooth candy coating off each square and lined the grey lumps up on the windowsill. How ugly and completely inedible they looked.

Another time I took the eye of a halibut my mother was preparing for dinner (in those days one bought whole fish) and brought it upstairs to the training potty, dropping it into thc puddle of urine and calling my mother to see what I had wrought. She was horrified, not seeing a halibut eye but thinking I had lost some bizarre interior part. I recognized her vulnerability as a warning to be more secretive about what I did, an impression that carried into adult life.

My mother, who loved the outdoors, and whose favorite book was Gene Stratton-Porter's *Girl of the Limberlost,* took me for a walk in a swamp. It was necessary to jump from one hummock of swamp grass to another. I was terrified of the dark water distance between these hummocks and finally stood marooned and bawling on a quivering clump, unable to make it to the next one.

We had a green roadster with a rumble seat where I usually rode in solitary splendor, then with my little fox terrier, Rinty, later run over by a motorcycle he was chasing. In this roadster one time my mother was stung by a yellow jacket and I wept for her. She had blood on her skirt, probably from her period, but I, connecting cause and effect, thought the wasp had caused her to bleed.

The hurricane of 1938 arrived when my twin sisters, Joyce and Janet, were only a few months old. The wind increased, shaking the small house. I don't know where my father was, probably at work. We had no telephone, no radio. My mother decided we should take refuge at a neighbor's house down the road. We walked, my mother burdened with boxes and a suitcase and one of the twins. Although I was barely three I had the job of carrying the other twin. At the neighbor's house I remember the moaning wind and the French doors that suddenly began losing panes of glass, and men hammering boards over the outside of the glass doors, making the house gloomy as well as strange.

My mother came from a large rural family of five girls and four boys. A few years after the hurricane we moved to a house in Plainfield, Connecticut, a house that belonged to my mother's parents, Lewis and Sarah (Geer) Gill. My mother's antecedents, the Gills, Geers and Crowells, came from longtime farm people who began to be absorbed into the textile industry in the nineteenth century. The Crowells had an artistic bent; one was a master furniture maker, another created stencils for the decorative panels of Hitchcock chairs. During the time we lived in the Plainfield house, my father was abroad, helping set up a textile mill in South America.

This roadside house had been a gas station at one time, one of several of my fertile-minded grandfather Gill's business ventures. He had invented devices for textile machinery that made him no money at all, then started the gas station and, a few years after we lived in it, converted it to a fabric and mill-ends shop. He could fix anything and was a skilled carpenter. These grandparents, whom the children and grandchildren alike called Ma and Dad, had a huge garden where I loved the exotic husk tomatoes, peeling their papery covers away and eating the sweet-tanged fruits. Dad had a grumpy old dog named Duke. There were a few cows that my uncles had to tend and an electric fence around the garden. My cousins and I thought it was fun to make a human chain, one grasping the electric fence, the one on the end getting the magnified jolt.

My maternal grandmother, Ma, née Sarah Mayo Geer, was descended from two orphan brothers who came from Heavitree near Bristol, England, to Connecticut in 1635. She always seemed harassed by her large family of children, and with so many people swarming in and out, the house was less tidy than comfortable. She washed and ironed her paper money so it would be crisp. She may have starched it. She was impatient, but a sucker for kitchen gadgets and an inventive storyteller with a grand sense of humor and at one time wrote a newspaper column. The family, being what it is, has always assigned my interest in books and writing to Ma's influence. Why not? Others in the family have written books and essays as well; my uncle Ardian Gill wrote a novel about John Wesley Powell's journey down the Colorado River. Cousin David Robinson wrote for *National Geographic* for years. Music and art and crafts were strong interests. My mother and her sister Gloriana (everyone had two or three nicknames and we called her Hikee) painted. The oldest sister, Sarah, got greatly involved in tinsel painting and resurrected the stencils of their great-uncle, Bill Crowell. All of them sewed their children's clothes. My mother had a loom and wove rugs. My sisters and I grew up accepting the making of things as normal. For years I sewed my own clothes until computers made sewing machines so complicated and cranky that the fun was gone.

The Gill house, which my grandfather and uncles built, seemed always in exciting turmoil, someone always searching for something misplaced, and on the stair landing there was a fabulous window set with panes of colored glass. I gazed through it to see the world shift to deep red, sickly orange or an unnatural green.

Before I started school my mother, my twin sisters and I lived in a small log cabin surrounded by big pines at the back of my grandfather's property. To this day the smell of white pine instantly sweeps me back to childhood with a sense of sadness and inchoate longing. The log cabin period may have been before the twins were born. I don't trust the tricks of memory. My mother and her brothers had built this cabin, probably a dream of her *Girl of the Limberlost* days. There was an old wax cylinder player in the cabin. My mother wound up the crank, the cylinder revolved and the story of The Three Bears emerged in a tinny voice.

One cabin window faced west framing a hill that had burned

years before. The black tree snags silhouetted against the sky looked like deformed giraffes and skeletal elephants. They seemed both sad and frightening. In the deepening twilight the bony creature shapes seemed to move, the twitch of a leg, a neck bent. Today, in the summer twilight at Bird Cloud, the greasewood and rabbitbrush hunch themselves into giant marmots, crippled elk. The most beautiful object in my mother's cabin was her cerulean blue silk brocade robe, a present to her from my father. Burning with fever one winter night she walked barefoot out into the snow dressed only in this lovely garment. Later someone said she had pneumonia, a disease she harbored many times in her life.

At some point we moved out of the cabin and into my grandfather's ex–gas station, rejuvenated as a house. I remember the boredom of obligatory nap time and the pattern of cracks in the ceiling, the nasty yellow marshmallow chickens that sugared our shoes on Easter morning. I remember waking up once in darkness and feeling something sticky and hot on my ear, being conscious of a creature leaping away. It was a rat and it had bitten me. Only the scar and the memory remain. Although my grandparents and great-grandparents were close by, and aunts, uncles and cousins constantly visiting, I had a sense of aloneness, of not being part of the buzzing hive of relatives. Old Duke killed my small kitten and I was outraged that he was allowed to go on living as though nothing had happened. I would have appreciated a trial, a jury, and a death sentence.

My mother loved to sunbathe and would lie motionless for hours on a blanket in the hot, weedy sun, her closed eyes covered with two green leaves. We had a pet crow (called Jimmy after the Civil War song refrain "Jimmy crack corn and I don't care"). He was inquisitive and would sidle up to my mother on her towel and carefully remove each leaf. He was reassured that she was not dead when she opened one of her green eyes. When my mother built a stone fireplace in the backyard I was allowed to press my hand into the wet, gritty concrete that had not yet set and the crow walked about in it leaving his prints as well. Years later, as we were moving from 2217 McBride Avenue in Utica, New York, in a car packed to the roof with kids and clothes, my father put Jimmy in a hole-punched cardboard box, and lashed the box to the back bumper. The poor fellow was dead when we stopped for lunch by the side of the road, asphyxiated by exhaust. I never forgave my father for this crime. The misfortunes that befell loved pets were my introduction to tragic and inconsolable loss.

We moved and moved and moved. Over the years we lived in dozens of houses. A place in Rhode Island had the outline of someone's arm in the broken sheetrock at the bottom of the stairs. A house in Black Mountain, North Carolina, offered a good view of shade trees where chain gang road crews rested. A place in Maine had beautiful elms whose roots swelled up near the surface and made mowing the lawn difficult. Then the Maine Turnpike went in a quarter of a mile away and almost immediately there was a ghastly accident that brought police, rescue vehicles and the too-late ambulance. An official state cross indicating a death had occurred at this spot went up, a safety warning policy the state of Maine dropped when the proliferation of crosses along the highway gave it a ghoulish appearance.

A large part of the reason for constantly moving was my father's obsessive desire to escape his French Canadian heritage and reinvent himself as a New England Yankee, to escape working-class poverty, to achieve financial success, to climb the ladder into the safe middle class. He and his family were victims of the racism that infected the dominant culture of white, Anglo-Saxon Protestant New Englanders, who saw immigrants, especially French Canadians from the north, as racially inferior. Less overt now, white racist anxiety persists in that area. I think an important factor in why my father married my mother—they were ill-suited to each other—was my mother's old New England family, poor but with the superiority of early arrival, just fifteen years behind the *Mayflower*. They never accepted him, of course—how could they? A son-in-law with the flamboyant middle name of Napoleon! The genealogical scratching around we've done has turned up more florid French names in his forebears, such as Dieudonné, Narcisse, Norbot and Ovila, which make George Napoleon sound rather tame. Still, they tolerated him and us and we all pretended to be a family honoring equality and diversity.

Growing up we knew very little about my father's family and rarely spent time with them. His mother, Phoebe Brisson Proulx Maloney Carpentieri, married three times: a French Canadian (Proulx), an Irishman (Maloney) and an Italian (Carpentieri) from Napoli who taught my father to make spaghetti sauce—a sauce which I and my sisters all make today, our best, perhaps our only, gift from a hard-to-know father.

So there were mysteries for us. There was some talk from our father that we were part Indian, but he believed the proof had been in the trunk of his grandmother Exilda (a.k.a. Maggie), which disappeared after her death and never resurfaced. The only evidence was his mother's smoky skin color and a few imaginative newspaper stories. There were other intriguing stories, such as one about a growth on our grandmother Phoebe's nose, a voyage across "the river" (the St.-Laurent always imagined) to an Indian settlement where a shaman or medicine man removed the growth in some unspecified manner. Our pleas to our father and to his mother, Phoebe, for details and enlightenment were never satisfied. Anonymity seemed the goal, but these half-stories were fuel on the fire of our longing to know more.

This attachment to clan ancestors seems to characterize all humans, and the ancient stories told about the departed— embroidered and amplified—were perhaps the rudimentary sources of history and of fiction. Certainly the Romans them-selves were keenly reverent of their ancestors, polishing the links to old families, the ideal the Gracchi, founders of Rome in 753 B.C., or even the more ancient Etruscans who lived in cen-tral Italy before Rome. When Ötzi, the Neolithic–Copper Age man, was discovered in a melting glacier in the Alps in 1991, his mitochondrial DNA analysis showed he was in a subhaplogroup called K1. (There are three K1 subhaplogroups.) Roughly 8 per-cent of today's Europeans also belong to the K1 haplogroup. Many then believed they were descended from Ötzi. Extremely cool to have a five-thousand-year-old ancestor with a stone arrow point in his back. But further DNA testing reports in 2008 showed that Ötzi belonged to a different subhaplogroup, one unknown before the advanced analysis. It is now called "Ötzi's branch" and apparently this haplogroup—his genetic group— has disappeared from the human genome. It may be extinct or exceedingly rare. Now no one is known to have Ötzi as an ancestor—one of the disappointments of science.

For me, many years later, an atmosphere of specialness still hovers over the extended maternal family like some rare per-fume that nearly four hundred years of New England resi-dence emits. I imagine this aroma compounded of fresh milk, split oak wood, autumnal leaves, snow, muggy swamps, pho-tograph albums and cold ashes.

CHAPTER 2

A Yard of Cloth

In the late 1980s on the day after Thanksgiving my younger sister Roberta and I went to visit our mother in her little apartment complex of housing for the elderly in Bristol, New Hampshire. At the time we both lived in Vermont on the west side of the Connecticut River. The day was mild for late November, heavy overcast, light rain and fog, one of those dark days that New England breeds in autumn. There were deer hunters on the road driving at twenty miles per hour, craning their necks to see into the scraggy woods.

Roberta and I are close in the sense that we often think and feel in similar ways. At that time we tried to visit our mother, Lois Gill Proulx, once a month. She had been ill for years with bronchiectasis, an uncommon degenerative lung disease which she fought with exercises, diet, medication and willpower. Frequent bouts of pneumonia and colitis attacks lurked as accompanists. Her closest sister, Gloriana (beloved Hikee), had the same miserable disease and in the summer of 2008, my cousin Eleanor Goodenough Milner and I, going through some of my mother's papers, came upon a poignant and upsetting correspondence between the two sick sisters. The sense of the hopelessly brave front, the running jokes, the closest sisterly bond, a hatred for stupid and condescending doctors—of all the things two people suffering the same illness can say to each other that no one else could understand—overwhelmed us. I can now barely open the box that holds those letters because all the disappointed dreams of these two hungry-for-love women fly in my face.

On that post-Thanksgiving day Roberta and I drove into the gathering gloom of Bristol. On the corner, a block from our mother's building, there had once been a wonderful rock shop full of minerals, geodes, bits of agate, amethyst crystals, odd mudstone shapes, slabs of malachite. But the sign was gone and in its place was a drooping banner in the window: DECORATOR FABRICS LOWER THAN WHOLESALE. Roberta and I both like beads, cloth, yarn, needles.

"Let's look on the way back if they're still open."

"Yes."

The dinner was pork loin, creamed onions that tasted exactly the same as they had when we were children, sweet potato, applesauce Roberta had made from a neighbor's apples, swapping him a chicken. Our mother was tired, but in fairly good health and spirits. She had exhausted herself for two days making the dinner. (Guilt! Guilt!) My mother and I each drank a glass of wine.

Late in the afternoon we left her. The light was fading. A thin mist blurred the small branches of the trees. At the corner we remembered the fabric sale sign. The place was still open. I parked the truck and we went inside.

There was no one in the shop. No one. Piles of folded fabric were stacked on long tables, bolts of shimmering brocade leaned against the wall. The shop stank of old minerals, stale cigarette smoke and the scent of wet leaves and rain we brought in with us.

The bolts of fabric were as awkward as loose walking sticks and slid and fell against each other when we tried to pull any one out. It was difficult to see the patterns without knocking down a dozen of them. As we wrestled with the slippery bolts the door opened and a man came in.

In some inexplicable way he was repellent. His face was creased and seamed, his black hair combed over a narrow skull. Slack stubbled cheeks, discolored teeth. The bolts of fabric seemed viciously animated. The man began to talk to us in an obsequious, intimate tone of voice. His comments were inane, stupid.

"I know ladies like to rummage around with cloth."

The damn bolts of designer fabrics, probably hijacked, I thought, refused to stay in place. The man asked us where we came from. We evaded, saying simply "Vermont" and "across the river."

"Where in Vermont? What town?" He would not give up.

"Oh, central Vermont, around Montpelier," I lied.

Now he insisted we take his business card. The cards were just across the street in his antique shop. No, no, we didn't want him to bother. We refused. I was suddenly wild to get away from this man. He began to wind clocks, set the hands. I hated him. The fabrics were rich and fine, the prices very low, but it was impossible to make a rational selection with the man talking on and on in his oily way. Snatching up a bolt of fabric without looking at it I said I would take a yard of cloth, try it at home and see if the colors were right. Anything to get away.

He produced a grimy yardstick from under the counter and a pair of scissors with a broken point. My sister leaned silently over an empty birdcage still encrusted with droppings. With a little flourish, and promising "I'll give you more than a yard," the man measured, cut briefly with the scissors, then tore the fabric and folded it into a small square. In the exchange of money his hand—very graceful and long-fingered—touched mine. Fever hot.

Yet we still could not get away. A barrage of advice to drive carefully, to take care, warnings that it was a bad night, there was fog, the road was slippery followed us down the steps. I thought his persistence extraordinary. Finally, alone on the sidewalk, we told each other that we had had a singular encounter.

We drove west through the mist and damp. The light was a somber, northern grey, the road blurred with light rain. Fog hung over the Pemigewasset. On the outskirts of town the road widened. We were alone on the highway. My sister was reading a letter. We came into the broad, sweeping curve that follows the river's course. In front of us, skewed across the empty road, in the smoking-grey silence were two smashed grey cars, pillars of steam rising from each, the road a fine carpet of glass. We stopped. Silence, stillness, all as static as a stage scene. There seemed no one in the terribly smashed cars, all the vehicles' glass on the road, the metal torn and compressed. A broad red runner of radiator fluid glistened on the wet road. We went to the cars. I could see a slumped figure.

Other vehicles began to come up behind us, most of them pulling around and continuing on their way. A pickup stopped. Two young men leapt out and began to pull at the farther crashed car's door.

"Don't move them," I called.

Their hands withdrew from something, someone. My sister and I were at the nearer car. We saw the humped man, the blood, we saw he was young with thick, light hair, the brilliant red soaking into a blond mustache, something on the seat beside him like a brace, some plastic soda bottles. He moaned. My sister touched his shoulder. His face was grey, his eyes closed. His clothes sparkled with glass. He made a twisting hunch. His legs rattled. My sister's hand lay lightly on his shoulder.

Now cars were coming from both directions, swerving and cutting around or pulling over, the people getting out to stare. No police.

"I'll go for help," I called to the young men.

"The police station!" they yelled back. "Half a mile down the road."

"Don't move, we'll get help, help is coming," I said to the injured man. I doubted he heard me. I ran to my truck, looked back. My sister was still with him, her hand on his shoulder. I called to her. She stepped toward me, turned back to the injured man, again stepped toward me, but reluctantly, still looking at him, her hand still outstretched even as she came away from him as though she couldn't bear to leave him. A few days later we learned he had died from his injuries.

At the station the dispatcher called for police, ambulances, the Jaws of Life, fire trucks, someone to control traffic. In minutes flashing lights and sirens went by. We did not go back to the scene but headed home by another, longer road, many miles out of our way and clogged with traffic crawling through the thickening fog. I drove slowly and carefully.

My sister and I both believed the man in the shop had saved our lives with his delaying talk, his cautions. A minute or two earlier and it could have been us wrecked on the curve of the river road. It was a singular and disturbing incident and we both felt its importance.

That night I telephoned my mother and told her about the

accident and about the man in the shop who gave us the creeps but had perhaps saved us.

"Ah," she said. There was a note of contemptuous amusement in her voice. "You know what his name is, don't you, the man in the shop?"

"No. He wanted to give us his card but I didn't take it."

"His name is Proulx," she said. In her tone—or did I misinterpret?—was her family's careful Yankee neutrality toward my father which I had come to see as rejection. This disclosure had the effect of an electric shock. The private questions welled. My sister and I spoke intensely to each other. The silence of our childhood, adulthood, suddenly broken. Who was this man with our name? Who were we? Who were our people? We knew so little. The American experience, the focus on individual achievement, the acquisition of goods and money to prove one's social value, is built on this sense of loss, this alienation from the warmth of the home culture, isolation from genetic bonds. This separation from one's tribe creates an inner loneliness that increases as one ages. There is in many people, especially immigrants, a burning need to complete the puzzle, to find the missing pieces. And what did it do to us, growing up as outsiders, as part of no place—we had moved more than twenty times by the time I was fifteen—as part of no people except our mother's pale-eyed Yankee clan who subtly gave us the sense that we were different and somehow tainted? Now we regret not speaking with the man who shared our name.

I have moved countless times in my adult life, too. Part of this peripatetic behavior is because Americans are a mobile people, but I also come from a Franco American background, rootless people who have no national identity, who really belong nowhere in the United States. The groups closest to fitting in I suppose are the French in Maine who have chipped out a place, and the French from the Canadian Maritimes who, after the 1755 expulsion from Acadia, went to France where they were not welcomed, then to Louisiana where they became Cajuns (a corruption of the word "Acadians"). The places and habitations where we live have histories, though we rarely know them.

We slide into houses and apartments others have built and rarely have a clue about what went on there, if the first owner grew an orchard of cherries and pears, how came that bizarre stairway with risers of varied heights, if that large piece of slate in the backyard was a wolf stone, if Indians knew the place and what they did there. I wondered about those things as my family moved and moved again around New England, leaving our hearts in Vermont, on to North Carolina, then again in Maine, but not belonging to any of those places. Jack Kerouac nailed it when he wrote of "that horrible homelessness of all French-Canadians abroad in America."[1] There was one year in my life when I lived in Montréal, and several when I commuted there from Vermont to graduate school, picked up a little *joual,* became familiar with the flat riverine landscape and the shapes of faces. Years later came a weekend in my life when I went to a gathering of Franco American writers on an island in Maine. As I walked into the room I was slammed with the shock of recognition. Here were non-Anglo people, people with familiar lineaments, with long fingers and slender bones, with dark eyes and hair and certain ways of moving and gesturing. Tears came to my eyes and for a little while I felt the curious but lovely sensation of being with the home herd and fantasized moving to Québec, Montréal or the Gaspé or Mont-

1. Jack Kerouac, letter to Yvonne Le Maitre, a critic-journalist who wrote for Québec publications, September 8, 1950. I am indebted to David Plante for the quotation, and to Isaac Gewirtz of the New York Public Library, who tracked down the source.

magny. But by then I had been too long in solitude, too anglicized for the joy to last.

In 1993, plagued by questions of family origins, I engaged Diane L, a genealogical researcher in Connecticut, to see what she could find out about my father's tangled family and whether or not the Indian connection was real and, if so, what tribe or group. Over the next few years she checked birth and death records, consulted voluminous tomes of records on immigration, baptism, marriages, births, federal census reports, sextons' reports, corresponded with genealogical societies. For the Canadian end of the research Richard De Gruchy, a Montréal genealogist, discovered relatives whose names I had never heard. I found it all confusing, a total overload of statistical information about too many people. It seemed such a shifting, murky compilation of hundreds of people, that I felt quite overwhelmed as though I had been dropped into Peter Matthiessen's *Lost Man's River* as one of the multitude of estranged, wandering but related characters.

The branches of my father's family seemed to boil down to my father's mother, Phoebe Brisson, daughter of Olivier (Levi) Brisson and Exilda (Maggie) LaBarge, and my father's father, Peter Ovila Proulx, born in 1886, son of Michel Preault [*sic*] and wife Melina. New England clerks mangled French names and struggled hopelessly with Québec place names and all of these had multiple variations of spelling. St.-Rémi south of Montréal became St Remal, or St Remic, Canada. It seemed all members of the various family clans married three or four times, all had nicknames as well as "*dit*" names, all used Americanized forms of their birth names. They had enormous families with many infant deaths, often renaming new babies after those who had died. But gradually some clarity emerged.

My grandmother, Phoebe Brisson, was also descended from the LaBarges. The LaBarge connection led back to Robert Laberge of Normandy, "a native of Columbière in the diocese of Bayonne" born in 1633. He came to Québec and settled in Montmorency where he married in 1663. His great-great-grandson, Joseph Maria LaBarge, born in L'Assomption, Québec, in 1787, left home in 1808 at age twenty-one. Hiram Chittenden wrote:

> He traveled by the usual route, up the Ottawa River and through the intricate system of waterways in northern Ontario which leads to Georgian Bay and to Lake Huron. Thence he went by way of Mackinaw Strait and Lake Michigan to Green Bay, and along the Fox and Wisconsin rivers to the Mississippi, which he descended to St. Louis. He used a single birch-bark canoe all the way, with only eight miles of portaging.[2]

In St. Louis he married "a Creole descendant of both the Spanish and French elements in the settlement of the Mississippi Valley" in 1813.[3] Later he answered a newspaper advertisement calling for one hundred good men to trap fur in the American west. So he became a member of General William H. Ashley's fur expedition of 1828, and a western Wyoming stream, La Barge Creek, near the town named La Barge, now bears his name. His name was attached to the creek and the town because of reports that he was scalped there by an Arickaree camping with or near the trappers. Although James Cly-

2. Hiram Martin Chittenden, *History of Early Steamboat Navigation on the Missouri River: Life and Adventures of Joseph La Barge Pioneer Navigator and Indian Trader for Fifty Years Identified with the Commerce of the Missouri Valley* (New York: Francis P. Harper, 1903), 1:3.
    3. Ibid., 1:2.

man and that wild liar James Beckwourth said that LaBarge had been killed, he was not killed.[4] Hiram Chittenden, in his biography of the son, Captain Joseph LaBarge, reports that the father carried a tomahawk scar on his head—perhaps from the Wyoming attack, although he was in other Indian fights on the Missouri. On that first westering trip Ashley's notes refer to the bluff west of Pass Creek to the south of Elk Mountain. Although there is no way to be sure, if the trappers were following the North Platte, that bluff was probably Bird Cloud's cliff, a notable landmark.

Joseph Maria returned to St. Louis, took up charcoal making, ran a boardinghouse and recruited young men for Ashley's fur-trapping enterprises. He fathered seven children. Three sons, Joseph (b. 1815), Charles S. and John B., were all steamboat captains. Joseph at age seventeen bound himself for three years to Pierre Choteau's ruthless American Fur Company as "voyageur, engagé, or clerk," advanced rapidly to steamboat captain with a deep knowledge of the great river's shifting channels.[5] He became celebrated as the premier Missouri pilot and is said to have influenced Mark Twain's knowledge of steamboat captains.[6] In his first year of employment he spent the winter of 1832–33 in a Pawnee village in the vicinity of Council Bluffs, learning the language and ways of the tribe.

In 1837 the American Fur Company's ill-starred steamboat

4. Charles L. Camp, "James Clyman," in *The Mountain Men and the Fur Trade of the Far West*, ed. LeRoy R. Hafen (Spokane: Arthur H. Clark Co., 2003), 1:244. *The Life and Adventures of James P. Beckwourth*, written from his own dictation by T. D. Bonner (New York, 1856), 63.

5. Chittenden, *History*, 1:23.

6. For the best information see Chittenden, *History*, vols. 1 and 2. Paul O'Neil, *The Rivermen* (Alexandria, Va.: Time-Life Books, 1975), confuses the father, Joseph Maria LaBarge, with his son, the steamboat captain Joseph LaBarge. The result is snappy adventure rather than carefully checked history.

St. Peter's brought smallpox to the Mandans on the upper Missouri and lit the disease fire that decimated the western tribes in the following decades. LaBarge was not involved in this horrific encounter—Bernard Pratte, Jr., captained the *St. Peter's* on that trip. But LaBarge had his own experiences of epidemics. In 1833, in his second year of employment with the American Fur Company, he was on board the *Yellowstone* captained by Andrew Bennett. On board as passengers were the German naturalist and early ethnographer, Prince Maximilian of Wied, and the Swiss painter Karl Bodmer. A cholera epidemic was roaring through the country and broke out aboard the *Yellowstone*. The crew was hard-hit and Bennett was forced to go back to St. Louis to find new men, leaving the *Yellowstone* in the hands of young LaBarge. Local residents came to the riverbank and shouted that if the boat did not leave the state of Missouri immediately they would set it on fire. Both the fireman and the engineer were dead. Eighteen-year-old LaBarge fired up the boiler alone and navigated the boat to the west shore above the Kansas river. His reputation was made.

He alternately worked for the American Fur Company or quit them to make his own way, suffering several financial disasters. During his career LaBarge knew many of the famous people of his time. As a young boy he met Lafayette. Audubon—whom he disliked—was once his passenger as were the Jesuit missionaries Fathers Christian Hoecken and Pierre-Jean De Smet.[7] He knew Brigham Young. Although Captain LaBarge's brother Charles died in 1852 in a steamboat explosion and brother John collapsed and died while making a boat landing at Bismarck, North Dakota, thirty-three years later,

---

7. Father Hoecken, after ministering to stricken passengers, died in 1851 on board the *St. Ange* during a cholera outbreak. Father De Smet who was also on board and ill with "bilious fever" survived.

Joseph LaBarge lived to be eighty-four, an illustrious St. Louis citizen, dying in 1899. When I sent my father this information he had no comment. It might have mattered to him when he was a child, but not when he was close to his nineties.

The Brisson connection was less glamorous. Three early Brissons came from France to New France. Only one of them settled in the Laprairie–St.-Constant–St.-Rémi area—Sebastien Brisson *dit* Laroche, and according to the gencalogist Richard De Gruchy, who worked on our problem, all the Brissons of St.-Rémi were descended from Sebastien, born around 1671 in Bordeaux, Guyenne, France. He married Marie-Marguerite Larivière in June 1722 in Québec.

Although I give little credence to the family belief in an Indian connection, I can see how descendants thought the Brissons were the link. Olivier, or, as he called himself, "Levi" Brisson, my father's maternal grandfather, came from St.-Rémi, a rural Francophone village in Napierville County south of Montréal, to Connecticut in the 1860s. St.-Rémi is near Kahnawake, the northern New York State Mohawk reserve on the St. Lawrence River. Levi settled in East Killingly, Connecticut, on the Rhode Island border and gained considerable local fame claiming to be the father of forty or more children with three wives, all scattered in a trail from Québec to Minnesota to Connecticut. Several interviewers took down his story (reproducing his broken English in the standard caricature of the little French Canadian). We hear his voice:

> I know I have feefteen child leeveing, how many more in Minnesota, Canada, y'odder place, O do not know. One time a was a well off, but a have so much seeckness, so many funeral, eet make me poor. Mon dieu, when a feller raise t'ree beeg fam' like a raise, she don' save much eef she leeve on farm. In se fac-

tory eet ees differaint. A feller she can put hees boys and girls in ze mill an save money 'n bimeby she kin go back to Canada and leave on her fa'm. Zat leetle girl here's ze youngest one. Ma wife, he have one m' but she ain't leeve. She bo'n dead and she have no place in ze church."[8]

From a cousin in Florida I have a copy of a photograph that shows the hawk-faced little man, reported to weigh only 110 pounds, sitting on his doorstep with five of his children. Strings of dried apples, which my relative was pleased to call bear claws, hung on the side of the house. My grandmother, about five years old, sits in the front row. At the time of the interview Levi Brisson was reputedly between eighty and ninety years old. They were living rent-free in an old schoolhouse by agreement with the school district. The Brisson children would maintain the pupil population necessary to keep another school and teacher going in accordance with Rhode Island regulations.

Monsieur Brisson and his family are not squatters, as they have been represented, or misrepresented. They are, it is true, living on a part of the public domain, occupying a public mansion, but they are giving an equivalent, which, instead of making them, as they have been made to appear, semi-paupers, makes them really public benefactors, inasmuch as their accession to the district population makes possible the continuation of a seat of learning within its borders.[9]

The articles provide most of what we know about this man. *The Providence Journal* reporter paraphrased him as saying "he

8. "Father of Forty, Monsieur Brisson, the French-Canadian Patriarch in Foster," *Providence Sunday Journal,* June 3, 1903.
9. Ibid.

was born in the parish of St. Remick [St.-Rémi], near Montréal, in 1820, but could not recall the day of the month. He had lived in the States more than 40 years, half of that time within a dozen miles or so of Danielson, Conn. He was married three times. His first wife, Clemence Benjamin, bore him six children, including one pair of twins. His second spouse, Mary Cyr, was the mother of 21, including two pairs of twins, and his third and pregnant wife, Maggie LeBarge, has borne him 11, of which four are dead."[10] If he had lived today he could have had his own television program.

Levi Brisson died five months after the interview, and the *Windham County Transcript* ran the following obituary:

> Levi Bresson [*sic*], whose familiar figure was so often seen on our streets, died at his home November [illegible]. He was a Canadian half-breed and his Indian blood was very conspicuous in his features and loping gait. He was born near Quebec between 80 and 90 years ago. He clung to his Indian habits of living and always seemed to prefer some little cabin for a home near the edge of a forest. Reporters have made him famous on account of the great number of his descendents, he being the father of 42 children. He was quaint and original in his sayings, voluble and social in his manner. The burial was Friday.[11]

However, newspaper reports are poor evidence, and the researcher Richard De Gruchy did not turn up any Indian connection at all, though speculating that because St.-Rémi was very close to the Mohawk Kahnawake Reservation perhaps the Brisson family had friends there, and "because of this

---

10. Ibid.
11. *Windham County Transcript,* November 19, 1903, 4.

somehow the notion of an Indian connection arose."[12] Diane L agreed that there was no solid proof of any Indian connection. Although several of his descendants, including my grandmother, my father and his cousin, Richard Brisson (a collector of Indian artifacts), believed in an Indian ancestor, the idea that Levi Brisson was a "half-breed" is not substantiated. My sisters and other relatives still hold onto the Indian ancestor.

Despite genealogical work in Connecticut and in Québec, Peter Ovila Proulx, my father's father, has not been tracked to his end and probably never will be. It no longer matters. My own father, George, said that he knew the man was lame, that he had had infantile paralysis as a child, that he was a skilled silk weaver. He always believed his father's family had come down from Trois-Rivières. The 1900 Connecticut census says Peter Ovila Proulx was then fourteen years old, could read and write, spoke English and was employed as a cotton spinner. He limped badly and was called "Turkey" Proulx because of his lurching gait. His World War I draft registration notes that he was short, had brown hair and eyes and was a "cripple." The divorce record says that Phoebe divorced him after three years of marriage "for habitual intemperance." From somewhere there came the unsubstantiated story that after the divorce he stole a locomotive and returned to Canada. No death records have turned up the name of this Ovila Proulx. There was a small flurry of excitement when a record of an Ovila Proulx from Woonsocket, Rhode Island, who fought in the First World War turned up, but the description did not fit. Peter Ovila simply disappeared, as so many men have done.

A child begins to think about his or her name and per-

12. Richard De Gruchy to Annie Proulx, May 6, 1996.

haps subconsciously reacts to it. Alan Lightman is a physicist-novelist; Raymond Seed became a biologist; there is a plants-man named Peabody and a rancher named Vaca. Jeffrey F. Brain chose psychotherapy as an occupation and Sonny Grouper was the developer of shark repellent. Oakes Ames (George Plimpton's grandfather) became a Harvard botanist. I do not know what Proulx (or Prou in the original form or Preault) means. No doubt there is a descriptor in genealogical name lists—some flattering phrase such as Brave-in-Battle or Stead-fast. I don't know.

Mr. De Gruchy backtracked Ovila to our original Jean Prou, the first ancestor to come to North America. "His name was Jean Proulx. He was the son of Jean Proulx and of Louise Val-lee of the parish of Notre-Dame-de-Nantilly, in the City and Arrondissement of Saumur, in the Bishopric of Angers, Anjou (today in the department of Maine-et-Loire), France and he arrived here sometime before 1672 for he married at Québec City on the 5 June 1673 to Jacquette Fournier."[13]

Although Jean Prou's employment contract has never been found, the census lists him as "a domestic in the service of Louis Couillard, Sieur de l'Espinay, Squire and Seigneur of Montmagny. Louis Couillard lived in the lower town of Qué-bec, on rue Notre-Dame. The house was full of people; 5 chil-dren between the ages of 2 and 14, the queen of the hearth, Geneviéve Després and two domestics, both named Jean. The two domestics, both 22 years old, were working out their indenture for the Seigneur. . . . Thus we may conclude that Jean Prou arrived in 1666, was 22 years old and worked as a household domestic."[14] After three years he was allowed to

13. Richard De Gruchy to Annie Proulx, November 25, 1996, 1.
14. Thomas J. Laforest, *Our French-Canadian Ancestors* (Palm Harbor, Florida: Quintin Publications), 3:216.

own less than three acres "comprised of high woods" on the river la Caille. For this he paid an annual homage to the seigneur of "1 sol in 'cens,' 3 live capons and 9 silver livres in 'rentes,' and 9 days of work on the seigneurie."[15] He also had to give one tenth of all the fish he caught to the seigneur, altogether rather tough terms. The land had to be cleared by hand, and he was still at it two years later. When, in February of 1671, Guillaume Fournier offered him 150 livres for his property he sold it and went back to Québec City. In 1672 Noël Morin, the seigneur of St.-Luc at Montmagny, granted Jean Prou some land at St.-Luc and an easier contract. He could keep his fish, but had to fell and cut four arpents of trees (an arpent is 0.85 percent of an acre) over the next year and live on the place as well. In 1673 he married Jacquette, the fourteen-year-old daughter of Guillaume Fournier. So he became one of the early settlers in Montmagny on the St.-Laurent. Jean Prou stayed in Montmagny.[16] The census of 1681 lists him as owning a rifle and twelve head of cattle and working six arpents of land. He and Jacquette increased the population of Montmagny with fourteen children. But something went wrong. The historian Thomas Laforest wrote:

> There is a twenty-year hiatus during which Jean Prou is never mentioned in official or civil documents. He surfaced on 14 October 1701, completely run down and out. Had he tried his hand in the fur trade? On his return to Québec, Marie-Anne Fortin, widow of Jean Picard, a provisions merchant, was waiting for him. She demanded, before the notary Chambelon, that

15. Ibid., 217.
16. Without knowing this I went for several summers to attend the famous Montmagny accordion festival while doing research for the novel *Accordion Crimes*.

he pay his debt of 700 livres and 16 sous for provisions furnished, which he admitted owing her. This debt was settled only after his death, from the proceeds of his estate.[17]

He died at age fifty-nine, March 1, 1703, leaving his widow with many children and a debt. She sold half the farm, including the house and barn, and moved in with her twenty-four-year-old son Joseph. The remaining assets were few—some land, one horse, one cow, three sheep, twenty-five chickens, four rifles, three sickles. By the time my father, George Napoleon Proulx, was born 250-odd years after his ancestor's arrival in the New World, all memory of Jean Prou had vanished from the family consciousness.

Through all of the Proulx baptism, birth, marriage, death records runs a black thread—"imbecile," "mulatto," "habitual intemperance," "her mark"—words one doesn't want to see in a family history, but they are there. It was a poor, mostly illiterate, rural clan of laborers unable to break out of the loop of continuing poverty and misery until my father, George Napoleon Proulx, managed it. Maybe he was right to put behind him all blood ties, to forgo the history, the Québec language, culture and religion, to make his own world as so many Americans have done. I don't think any of his children understood how he saw himself, his ambitions, his life.

The Chicano word "*rasquache*" comes to mind. It has two meanings. The negative meaning is of poor, low-class, uneducated, disorganized and dirty people. The other meaning has been adopted by art critics to describe a vigorous Chicano sensibility, expressing resistance, resourcefulness and adaptability, irony and defiant energy. My father came from roots character-

17. Laforest, *Our French-Canadian Ancestors,* 20:219.

ized by the first meaning and reinvented himself as an upwardly mobile white-collar American. His perpetual toast—"here's to bigger and better jobs and more money"—was one man's version of the American Dream. My conjectures about our vague French Canadian connection and the immigrant experience in general led to research for the novel *Accordion Crimes*.

A year after our father died my sister Roberta found a report in a January 1889 issue of *The New York Times* headlined THEY LEFT HIM TO DIE. The event took place 117 years before my father's death in 2006.

MONTREAL, Jan. 10—Last Sunday the body of George Proulx was found completely frozen in the woods near St. Maurice and was conveyed to Piles, where the Coroner has opened an inquest, but it was adjourned till Jan. 17 owing to the absence of important witnesses. The whole story is strange and melancholy, and recalls the adventures of early colonizing times. About the end of last November the deceased went to work in a lumber shanty near the source of the St. Maurice River. He fell sick, and when it was found he could not recover, the overseer determined to send him to Three Rivers. Having no conveyance two men were sent to help the invalid.

They started at the time when the cold was the severest at the beginning of the Winter. A heavy fall of snow followed, and the trail became impassable, when the travelers were in the dreary district of Tuque, about 100 miles from their destination, with only a few scattered shanties on the way.

In the middle of the storm the two protectors abandoned their charge on the River Bauke and left him to die. The dying man made an attempt to follow, but he was overpowered by cold and buried in the snow.

When these two men arrived at Piles they said nothing of the incident, but suspicions arose and a searching party was organized. Sandy Adams and Hercule Deseletz of Rivière Aux Rats found the body and conveyed it on a litter to Piles.

The conduct of the two men has caused great indignation, and when inquiry was instituted they could not be found.[18]

This unknown George Proulx joins the man in the fabric shop as another family mystery.

18. *New York Times,* January 11, 1889.

CHAPTER 3

Lodgepole Pines and Houses

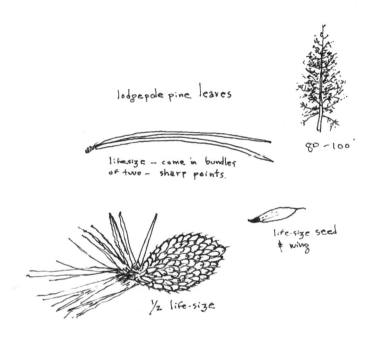

lodgepole pine leaves

lifesize — come in bundles
of two — sharp points.

80 -100'

life-size seed
& wing

½ life-size

2003–2004

God knows I had had plenty of experience of houses and apartments from New England to Newfoundland, North Carolina
to Japan, helped build several structures, rented some, bought
and sold others, renovated and endured. With Bird Cloud, I
saw the house rise from what I thought were good ideas. The
intentions were good at least. I still do not know where things

35

went wrong or even if they did go wrong. After years of wrestling with awkward domiciles I thought I knew what I needed in a house. I'm afraid I still don't know, which is another way of saying that for me there is no perfect house.

In the past there was a nineteenth-century farmhouse in northern Vermont with a collapsing shed reputed to have been the last-stand hideout for several Irish Fenians who came down from Canada to St. Albans, Vermont, during the uprising in 1866. When workmen were digging up the septic tank of this house one of them unearthed an 1860s dime—which he kept. Then there was the log house a friend and I built in Vermont's Northeast Kingdom, a wretched and weird semi-hippie building that cost much exhausting labor, from cutting the trees, limbing them, dragging them to the site, spudding the bark off, cutting the mortises and tenons for *pièce-sur-pièce* construction and putting the whole god-awful mess together. With the same friend there followed a sojourn in Montréal in the St.-Laurent district near the wonderful old market where one could buy road-stripe yellow chicken feet, exotic spices, little hot empanadas, durians and water chestnuts. We had a little apartment of strange angles in a house owned and run by a one-armed German ex-POW. An extremely tall transvestite who only wore summer dresses—inadequate for a Montréal winter—lived down the hall. The most memorable feature of this place was an ancient electric stove with heat coils lining the oven interior. I baked a cake in the oven once and the top coil hung down into the batter.

Later there was a converted bank vault, a rather dark place but certainly secure. Years of renovating a Newfoundland fisherman's house started with prying nineteen layers of linoleum off the rotten kitchen floor and ended seven years later with tears over the botched mess a local handyman made of the replacement floor. The first carpenter, who was an excellent craftsman, found a new sweetie on the Internet, left his wife and ran off to the mainland with the new love. And there was a short stay in what was probably in the 1960s a luxe house—it had sliding glass doors and a cottage cheese ceiling finish. Then there was a year or two in a Denver apartment with a view of a Ferris wheel and a nutcase on the top floor, and a little cabin without electricity on the Powder River in northeast Wyoming that came with an extraordinary sky. The Perseid meteor showers in August were the most stunning I ever saw, bushels of shooting stars, more than I could count. But coal trains rumbled through all night on the track a mile away. And then there was the house in Centennial, Wyoming.

In 1995 I bought a three-year-old log house in Centennial, a tiny town on the east slope of the Medicine Bow range in the southern Rockies. The elevation was eight thousand feet. West of the house was the national forest, steep slopes packed with lodgepole pine and threaded with hiking and ski trails. On the east reared the bulk of Sheep Mountain, a rugged chunk of mountain still populated by elk and mountain lions. Beyond that lay the Laramie plains where the Wyoming cattle business started after a nineteenth-century cattleman lost some of his cows on a drive from Montana summer pasture back to Texas. The next year, heading north with another herd, he discovered his lost cattle, fat, healthy and increased in numbers. From that time on, the Laramie plain with distant Laramie Peak on the skyline was cow country until very recently when a longtime ranch family sold out and small houses and a gas compression station sprouted up. I was glad not to live in one of these houses as the water table was expensively deep underground and the new house owners constantly had to haul in tanks of water.

Over the decade in Centennial I haunted the dark trails

summer and winter until I had explored most, skiing, hiking or riding my mountain bike on the old abandoned logging roads. In winter these same trails, so dramatically different under many feet of snow, became the best cross-country skiing of my life. I skied daily, sometimes only a few miles, sometimes for hours, depending on snow conditions. I saw few animals beyond birds and an occasional deer as this massive monoculture forest that lies between eight thousand and ten thousand feet was rather sterile for wildlife, a biological desert with virtually no understory. Only a few plants, such as the grouse whortleberry (*Vaccinium scoparium*) and elk sedge (*Carex geyeri*), grew in the dense shade. This open ground beneath the trees made walking anywhere easy in contrast to eastern forests with their thick bushy undergrowth and giant jackstraws deadfalls. In the Medicine Bows there was bear sign in the more remote draws and drainages, and Shiras moose in the swamps. I occasionally saw moose when skiing and remembered the way they ruined the few nascent cross-country ski trails in Newfoundland, their enormous hooves making deep holes in the ungroomed surface. It was better traveling if one got away from the ruined trail although the risk of getting lost in the tuckamore increased dramatically. In the Medicine Bows on a sunny day the black shadow stripes of the pines across a trail had a strobe effect that could be disorienting and even dangerous on steep, twisty runs.

Humans like lodgepole pines and have used them in dozens of ways. Because they grew so straight and tall many housebuilders liked them for post and beam structures. Indians used the younger, slenderest trees as tipi and travois poles. The pine pitch waterproofed moccasins and held feathers firmly in headdresses. The Cree reportedly used the gum in painful, hollow teeth to protect the nerves from exposure to the air. As a chewing gum it entertained the jaws and freshened the breath, and both Indians and settlers heated it and used it to ameliorate the itch of insect stings and bites, boils and ulcers. The bark, steeped in boiling water, made a scurvy-preventing brew that could be taken straight or mixed into stew and soups. Army doctors on the frontier learned to use the needles as a scorbutic.

I thought the Rocky Mountain lodgepole—sometimes called "black pine"—was beautiful in its great numbers but not deeply interesting until I started thinking about the cones and the red needles that even then were illustrating the great and terrible plague seizing the forest. The green forest itself was monotonous, mile after mile of the same trees, almost no diversity in age or in species. It was all lodgepole, and that was part of the problem.

The cones caught my attention first, cone-bearing end branches bitten off by squirrels who found it easier to cut the branch tips, watch them fall, then race down the tree and stockpile the nutritious cones under roots and fallen logs. I often saw their middens in the forest, huge heaps of discarded seed husks. One day I brought a squirrel-severed branch of the tightly closed, prickly cones home and left them on the big table. They were fastened asymmetrically so tightly to the branch that it was impossible to break or pull them off. For a few days they stayed as impregnable as clams, then started to open, spilling out their winged seeds, so like translucent insect wings, a pale brown the color of swamp water.

I learned that the lodgepole makes two kinds of cones— serotinous and nonserotinous. The nonserotinous, which was what I had brought home, open and scatter seed for the wind and squirrels every year. Young lodgepoles—ten to thirty years old—usually make these cones which open at temperatures of 79° to 125°F. Older trees, or trees in a region with a history of

fire, produce mostly serotinous cones which squirrels ignore
as too difficult, and which open only at higher temperatures
from 113° to 140°F.

The trees themselves were thin-barked and grew straight,
eighty to a hundred feet tall with branches that curved slightly
upward. They were the most common trees in the Rocky
Mountain west and gave the region its distinctive appearance. The stout needles came in bundles of two, each with a
long inner groove. Under my pocket microscope I saw chains
of transparent little bumps running the length of each and
assumed these were sacs of resin. I admired these lodgepole
pines that could so nimbly adapt their reproductive strategy,
and thought it illustrated the intermeshed flexibility of the natural world where call and response was the way of continued
life. There were many voices in this antiphonal choir: fire and
seed, disease and fire, sunlight and cutting, insect and beak,
parasite mistletoe and hungry squirrel. Although in the past
fire was sometimes an immediate enemy to specific stands of
lodgepole, fire also opened the serotinous cones and prepared
a nutrient-rich seedbed for the next generation. Those seedlings also had enemies: snowshoe hare, voles, the omnipresent
squirrels, pocket gophers and domestic cattle and sheep which
both ate and trampled leased forest sections. But the lodgepole
had no strategies or defenses against the triple catastrophes of
prolonged drought, warming climate and an unprecedented
invasion of mountain pine beetle, *Dendroctonus ponderosae,*
whose apt Latin name means "tree killer."

When I moved to Centennial, climate change in the Rockies
was taking the shape of a severe drought and shorter, warmer
winters without the prolonged deep temperatures of 30° to
40°F below zero that froze Wyoming in the past. This warming,
drying trend weakened the trees and was an important factor in

what has now become "the largest known insect infestation in the history of North America," the mountain pine beetle that has destroyed most of the lodgepole forests of the west.[1] Other conditions encouraged the invasion. As well as vast armies of monoculture trees, decades of fire suppression produced a susceptible same-age forest, the equivalent of a human population of millions of eighty-year-olds caught in the surge of a deadly infectious plague. And it was not just mountain pine beetles. Spruce bark beetles were after the spruce trees and fir engraver beetles were killing subalpine fir trees. Most of the lodgepole forests of Colorado and southern Wyoming are now standing dead. I am deeply sorry for all who never experienced the beautiful lodgepole forests of the American and Canadian Rockies, who never skied under the snowy branches or looked out from a fire tower across miles of green mountain wilderness. It is astonishing to me that so many people outside the west have no idea this has happened. Although many newspapers have reported the catastrophe, it remains something of a millions-of-acres secret.

The mountain pine beetle is a tiny creature that chews through a lodgepole's bark, gouges out a hollow in the wood and lays its eggs. The larvae hatch hungry and feed on the cambium layer, a tree's most vital part, the annual layer of cells that makes up a growth ring. To prevent drowning in the tree's sap, the beetle larvae can eject a choking fungus that not only halts the life-giving flow of sap, but stains the wood a grey-blue color. For a while furniture makers thought the blue wood was

---

1. Michael Ricciardi, "Massive Infestation of Beetles Threatens Mountain Pines in Western U.S.," July 22, 2009, ecolocalizer.com/2009/07/22/massive-infestation-of-beetles-threatens-mountain-pines-in-western-us; Jim Robbins, "Spread of Bark Beetles Kills Millions of Acres of Trees in West," *New York Times,* November 18, 2008, D3.

attractive, but it is now recognized as a disfigurement. Many people who cut lodgepole in the forest to heat their houses in winter brought the cordwood—and the beetles—into town. The beetles, delighted to have more food, moved into landscaped and ornamental trees. Lodgepoles have known beetle attacks before and their defense is a sticky, thick resin to swamp the beetles' egg galleries and holes. Unfortunately the beetles were stirred into pheromone action by this resin, sending out signals that attract myriad hordes of more attack beetles. Because of the long drought the dried-out and weakened trees were hampered in their resin defense.

The scourge covered virtually the entire west from British Columbia to New Mexico. British Columbia and Alberta had the worst infestations, but Wyoming, Colorado and Montana were hit a hard blow, millions of acres turned a dull rust-red. Predictions were that almost all lodgepole trees over five inches in diameter would be dead within the next few years. There was no known practical remedy. Today in the forests around Bird Cloud mile after mile of dead, red trees stand on their last roots and will eventually fall, making a terrifying pile of fire-ready timber. Once the fires begin perhaps even the East Coast will see the smoke.

Thinking about what comes afterward forces one to take the long view—how will the Rockies look in a hundred years, five hundred years? Will they come to resemble the Alps, rich in meadows and wildflowers? Will ranchers move in with cows? Will they look more like the deforested, erosion-clawed exposed steppes of Afghanistan? Will an embarrassed Forest Service embark on massive planting programs of diverse species? We don't know.

I should have learned all the important lessons about houses with the Centennial house. I learned some, but not enough.

The site was a two-acre lot, one of ten lots on ninety wooded acres managed by a homeowners' association. There was a half-mile access road which occasionally closed during heavy snowstorms. The house had plenty of problems, but the original builder was nearby and I embarked on a long series of improvements and repairs.

This entire house was heated with three electric "storage" heaters. The first winter proved they were utterly inadequate and stored nothing but expense. Rarely did the house temperature rise above 62°F, rather chill, and it was necessary to keep a wood fire burning in the stove. The kitchen was a beige horror, the tile floor and counters impossible to keep clean. This kitchen was cursed with mini cupboard space, an awkward layout and floor-to-ceiling east windows that in summer let in the intense high-altitude sunlight and converted the room into a glaring bake oven, a change from the winter freeze-out. Slowly, and painfully, as they began to fail, I discovered that the previous owners had bought the cheapest appliances possible. I had to replace the well pump, the washer and dryer. The electrical wiring was inadequate. Worst of all was the entrance to the garage, a smooth concrete slab on the north side and at the base of a slope. Every winter a thick glacier built up on the slab and extended about ten feet up the driveway. I spent many hours chipping at each winter's ice accumulation.

Renovation of this house began by covering the knotty pine ceilings with Sheetrock and putting a wood floor over the plywood. Each year, as I could afford it, there was a new project—bookshelves for my library, gutting of the kitchen and a full makeover, replacement of the electric heaters with a gas furnace, conversion of the unfinished basement to an office. I had the concrete slab in front of the garage ripped out and replaced with an underground heating system that almost worked, though it blew many fuses and bumped the electric bill up to national debt status, but it ended the glaciers. The new concrete apron had a rough finish to thwart the tendency of ice to cleave to smooth concrete.

When I first moved into this house the dark and unfinished basement was lined with rough shelves. A disturbing line about sixteen inches above the floor indicated a flood in the past. Driving through Clayton, New Mexico, I noticed the waterline high on a stone building from a flood in the 1920s and it reminded me of the basement's sinister watermark. It worried me. The house was situated at the bottom of a slope; on the hardened Wyoming clay, snowmelt water and rain ran rapidly over the ground in broad sheets without soaking in. All that saved the house from a yearly flood was a culvert under the driveway that led the upslope water safely away into an old irrigation ditch and the aspen grove below.

The flood situation became complicated by a Mr. Busybody neighbor who decided to block the irrigation ditch one autumn for reasons unknown. (There is a Mr. Busybody and a Mr. Know-All in every homeowners' association.) In the spring the water gurgled out from under the massive wind-driven snowdrifts to the west of the house, a permanent feature of living on the lee side of a mountain ridge. Inevitably water backed up and froze inside the culvert. By then Mr. B's ditch blockage work was buried under ten feet of ice and hard-frozen snow where I couldn't get at it to break through the choke point and divert the meltwater from the house. My oldest son and his wife came visiting for a weekend and we spent most of our time digging and hacking at the ice barrier. Everything froze up again as soon as the sun went down. As spring advanced, meltwater cascaded down the driveway and into the garage. To approach the house one needed mud boots and I put in hours digging diversion channels across the driveway. The situation could not be resolved amicably and to me it was clear that it was time to go.

No doubt about it, although the setting was exquisitely beautiful and near many miles of ideal mountain hiking, bicycling and ski trails, the house was wrong for me. During the frustrating time that I lived in it, I wrote an article describing what I thought was my ideal house. Even before the ditch blockage episode I had been looking for property on which I could build a house that would suit me. It took more than ten years to find what I believed to be the right place.

I looked nearby because I liked being close to the national forest and I liked Centennial, its funky main drag with an ancient police car parked near the highway to deter speeders, and, when I first arrived, five bars to serve a population of less than a hundred people. I looked at a property on flat prairie surrounded by a boulder field from an ancient local glacier. Under the house there was a half basement, a low room fitted with a workbench and storage shelves which one entered through a trapdoor; it was not possible to stand upright. I looked at another with every surface tiled to ward off dust. I admired a property to the southeast abutting another part of the forest until I learned it was a major revving-up zone for snowmobiles in winter, and I saw overpriced sage-land steppe, then some sloping land so high an oxygen mask would have been useful. Another piece was stratospherically expensive, ten thousand dollars an acre, located right on a heavily traveled highway, with restricted access and an allegedly grouchy neighbor. Finally I saw a handsome piece of property, private and beautiful with the North Fork of the Little Laramie River whisking through it and fine views of the north end of Sheep Mountain, and I could afford the price. I arranged to buy this forty-acre property, planning to build. Ten minutes before the time set for the closing the seller canceled out.

The search became desultory. In conversation with an acquaintance one day I said I had little hope of ever finding the right place. She asked if I had considered looking around the town of Saratoga on the North Platte River on the west slope of the Medicine Bow range. I said I thought that country very beautiful, but didn't think there was much for sale over there. No, she said, not much, but there was one place that might interest me. It belonged to The Nature Conservancy and they were looking for a buyer. It was on the river.

"It has big cliffs," she said. "And the river. You should look at it."

"I should."

A few weeks later I did look at it with the real estate agent who was handling the property. A bald eagle perched in a dead tree, watching us. The landscape was bold. Not only was the property on the North Platte River but the river ran through it, taking an east-west turn for a few miles in its course. The land was a section, 640 acres, a square mile of riparian shrubs and cottonwood, some wetland areas during June high water, sage flats and a lot of weedy overgrazed pasture. On the lower portion, about 120 acres, Jack Creek, an important spawning place for trout, came down from the Sierra Madre, thirty miles distant, and angled through the property to enter the North Platte. Jack Creek was big enough to need a bridge, and it had one, a sturdy structure made from the floor of a railroad freight car. The bulk of the property, more than five hundred acres, lay at the top of and behind the sandstone cliffs, a sloping expanse of sedge and sage. Top and bottom the land was seriously overgrazed and neglected, yet the day I first saw it I also saw a small herd of mule deer, pelicans, bald eagles, great blue herons, waterfowl, ravens, scores of bluebirds, a harrier, a kestrel, and, glued to the cliff, thousands of swallow nests. I knew most of Wyoming's wildlife kept to the riparian areas, but this was astonishing. The place was already a diverse wild-life habitat. It was obviously a refuge for birds and I thought at once that it could be managed as an avian preserve. It seemed wonderfully private, accessible only by a one-lane right-of-way. I didn't recognize the right-of-way lane as the property's Achilles' heel.

I learned that a rare plant, *Penstemon gibbensii,* grew high on the west end of the cliff among exquisite cushion plants and fossil coral, one of those natural rock gardens, although only ankle high, that make hiking the Rockies such a feast of beauty. The views on top took my breath away—and so did the wind. It was hard to stand up. I could see the great bulks of Coad, Pennock and Elk mountains to the northeast, and farther east my beloved Medicine Bow range, and to the southwest the Sierra Madre, called the "Shining Ones" by the Utes who once lived in them. The habitat at the top of the cliff was very different than at the base—grassland steppe, though overgrazed, showed a diversity of sedges and grasses. There was a small prairie dog town populated by extremely wary residents. A badger nose appeared briefly above a hole, then disappeared. A coyote slid into the distance. Down below a small herd of mule deer fording the river looked like toy animals. The property was beautiful and unique, remote and powerful, and I fell for it, hard. It was also unfenced, surrounded by cattle ranches, without electric or phone lines anywhere near. But I was in love.

The property had once belonged to a sheep ranch family with deep roots in Wyoming. The owner before The Nature Conservancy had planned a housing development. To that end a well had been drilled ten years earlier and a white plastic fence put up near the entrance, a kind of decorative flourish. There were also white-painted numbered stakes pounded into the ground to mark the long, skinny lot boundaries, each lot a mile deep and a few hundred feet wide, running across the sage-covered upland at the top of the cliff, straight down the four-hundred-foot face of the cliff, across the river and to the south property line so that the developer could claim each had river frontage. The arrangement might have been fun for Tarzan and Jane, who could have descended the cliff face on ropes and vines.

Buying this property, which came with a multipage conservation easement, was a lengthy process. There were many times when it looked as though it could not work out. But driving from Laramie to Centennial on a windy day when the sky was filled with stretched-out laminar wave clouds I saw to the west, in the direction of the distant property, one cloud in the shape of an immense bird, the head and beak, the breast looming over the Rockies. I took it as a sign that I would get the property and thought Bird Cloud should be the new name for the old sheep ranch.

There followed many months and vast quantities of paper and consultations with my lawyer, the State Board of [Water] Control, engineers, water testers, well drillers, the letter of intent, the purchase agreement, the reserved conservation agreement, appraisals, checking out of titles and quit claims, the well water analysis (so alkaline a new well and water treatment were necessaries), the easement documentation report, a new survey, a flood study report, gathering of the mineral rights information, and the Phase I environmental site assessment. It took six months before everything—money, paperwork, tests and measurements of all kinds, state permits—came together, but in December of 2003, at the title company in Rawlins, my children and I became the owners of Bird Cloud.

I knew I would work with an architect. The general approach to making houses in this part of the west is that it is the responsibility of the builder to translate the homeowner's ideas into reality without benefit of an architect. While this flatters the western claim to independent thinking and character, it sometimes results in quirky problem houses or repetitive buildings. At least that was my thinking at the time. That I was not entirely right became clear. If ever I have another house built I will consult a local architect with an office no more than twenty miles from the building site. I will put more value on the ideas and opinions of the construction crew. I will choose the appliances, plumbing and lighting fixtures myself.

I had corresponded with the architect Harry Teague over the years. His office was in Aspen, Colorado, which should have been the tip-off that he was hours away from Bird Cloud, too far for frequent site visits. Harry is a big, interesting, smart guy. I liked him and admired his house designs, especially one that resembled a metal slash in the tawny Colorado foothills. He liked rusted metal and salvaged materials as I did. He had a grand sense of humor and was sensitive to light and shadow, wind and rock.

In a kind of *via negativa* approach Harry and I went through the Centennial house and I pointed out the features that were problems I hoped never to encounter again: the lumpy log walls, the north-facing garage entrance, the ankle-to-ceiling east kitchen windows. I mentioned I had written an article about my dream house and he said he had read it. I was relieved to think that he already understood what I needed in a house. Later I decided that if he had read it he had quite forgotten the content. And when I reread it myself I saw it more as a complaint than as a constructive ideal.

Harry's first visit to the Bird Cloud site was on a day of

strong westerly winds that I assumed were an anomaly, but that he correctly perceived as the defining feature of the place. The cliff loomed, a dominating wall of buff stone. I eventually learned that the property was constantly assailed by strong winds sweeping in across miles of open and treeless grazing land to the west, their velocity increased by the channeling cliff. There are days when the whole country is stirred by lashing, tearing wind, the air thick with dust, microscopic particles of ancient ash and silt whisked aloft in towers. The faded grass is whipped by this wind and it thrashes to and fro as if activated by powerful jolts of underground electricity. Tumbleweed bounces across roadways, peppering the asphalt with its dark seed. This is the wind that batters I-80 twenty miles to the north and regularly hurls semi-trailer trucks onto their sides, as Newfoundland's Wreckhouse winds do on the western coast road. At Bird Cloud winds of seventy miles an hour are not uncommon in winter and blasts over a hundred miles an hour occur a few times each season, the source of the old joke that Wyoming snow does not melt, it just wears out. Those days are not days to hang out the laundry. Harry's design offered a narrow slanting roof to the west wind, guiding the roaring air smoothly up and over the house instead of letting it batter and slam full-on. The shape of the house roof echoed that of the backdrop cliff, something I always note with pleasure.

Because place is such a major part of my writing and life, I thought it important that Bird Cloud breathe in and out of the landscape, a house subject not only to the wind, but to the drowning shadows that submerge it every evening and the sharp slice of sunlight at the eastern end of the cliff. I wanted interesting pieces of light, sliver views as well as large windows holding the wide expanse of the cliff. Harry succeeded brilliantly with this, the variable and changing tones and shapes of light a constant pleasure. But it was also important that the big windows not lure birds to their deaths with inimical reflections. Harry's father, the industrial designer W. Dorwin Teague, whose work is featured in the Cooper-Hewitt National Design Museum in New York, suggested that set-back windows with an overhang would prevent bird deaths. It sounded like a good idea, and I still am not sure where or why that idea evaporated. Expense, no doubt, the factor which forced everyone's hand.

Lodgepole logs have been an indigenous and beautiful housebuilding material in the west for years, and the log house is the esteemed vernacular architecture of Wyoming. I admired an old log barn on a back road near Laramie and showed Harry a photograph of it. But I didn't want to live in a log house again unless the interior was drywalled, or the house built Québec style, *pièce-sur-pièce,* with squared logs. Interior walls of round, chinked logs are unattractive to my eye, and the uneven corduroy surface is impossible if you wish to hang paintings. The Centennial house taught me that interior logs are dreadful dust collectors. The twice-annual swabbing of the high, dust-laden logs in the Centennial house was work that never ended. Logs contract and expand according to humidity, temperature and season; the chinking material shrinks and insects pour in through tiny holes. Planed *pièce-sur-pièce* logs, though offering flat interior walls, still make for dark rooms and still need chinking. The heavy walls that result from using full logs are likely to sag and bow over time. Harry suggested we use two-inch-thick rough-cut planks cut with a slight taper to suggest *pièce-sur-pièce* construction, using a third of the material and less heavy labor. I agreed to this sensible idea. The exterior wood would be allowed to darken naturally, without stain.

Because I spend my life in a shifting welter of papers, books, letters, maps and schedule sheets, I perversely love a clean minimalist look. I especially admired the Langston Hughes Library in Clinton, Tennessee, designed by Maya Lin. It has taken me half a lifetime to understand that my habits and work do not tally with clean minimalism. By default, complexity and clutter are my style, and I move from projects and paper piles on one table to different projects and paper piles on other big tables. Books are open on every surface next to bins of papers to be filed. Boxes of old photographs, manuscript drafts, correspondence and receipts crowd shelves and floor. Incoming and outgoing mail piles up. This is not a svelte, minimalist look. One large room was what I thought I needed for the tables, file cabinets, map case, desks, shelves for books, office supplies, book accessioning station and bill-paying desk.

Adjacent to this library-office I hoped for a commodious kitchen with space for a sofa and chairs. I like to cook and cooking takes room for cleaning vegetables, prep work, chopping, slicing, for big pots, crocks and platters: paraphernalia, not minimalism. I wanted shelves for dozens of cookbooks. I grew up in rural New England in houses with large unheated pantries and knew their virtues. I wanted the kitchen door to lead to the vegetable garden. And because of the proximate river a fishing room seemed a marvelous addition, a place for rods and waders and nets just a minute away from the river and its dark pools.

As the design developed, there were compromises. The fishing room had to accommodate the laundry area and the storage of other sports equipment, flower presses, day packs, a sewing table, vases and a good deal of miscellany. The kitchen itself was smaller than I wanted, and a little more defined than open. But it is adjacent and open to the room with the big maple dining table where I often end up writing with quick access to hot pots on the stove, the view of the cliff and of bird behavior.

I wanted a modest but spacious bedroom with smooth ceilings and walls. The Centennial bedroom had five huge beams—each twelve to sixteen inches in diameter—across the ceiling and I would lie in bed staring up at them and wonder how quickly they would come down in an earthquake. It was not a bedroom with an excess of feng shui. I was keen to have tatami mats in a furniture-free alcove off the bedroom for meditation and exercise. I hoped for a commodious walk-in closet with good ventilation and a stupendous number of shelves and drawers. As I often travel, a small private attic for luggage and packing would be very useful.

The Centennial garage had been snug, but at least it had roomy storage cabinets and shelves. I hoped the Bird Cloud garage would hold two vehicles, an SUV for trips into Wyoming's backcountry, and a pickup to get around the property, to town and the dump. I hoped for a workbench and plenty of storage shelving. Underneath the master bedroom, Centennial had a noisy furnace, the replacement for the electric heaters, and I told Harry that a silent house was a major factor for me. I did not want to hear fans, blowers, pumps, whooshing and clunks.

The year turned the corner into 2004. As Harry and crew worked on the design, the search began for a local builder.

CHAPTER 4

The Iron Enters My Soul

gulls seem to feed on incoming tide.
piping plover likes the rockweed of low tide.

At low tide the 3 crows were down in the rockweed.
One gets sea urchin. picks out meat. How does he get it

One of the 3 crows that hang
out together has a white spot
on lower left neck area. Reminds
me of E T Seton's Silverspot. Have seen
it again + again.

light sand
color

piping ?
plover ?

2004

Harry Teague's first sketch for the house showed a long, dark building as lengthy as the old barn I fancied. There was no basement, a good idea as radon gas is a problem in this part of the world. The house was to be built on a slab with an interior ground floor of polished concrete. I had once mentioned to Harry that I was drawn to asymmetry in all things. So I was delighted to see the design was a long and narrow structure, but not a rectangle, incorporating interesting angles in its walls and the front and back entrances. The largest room, forty-eight feet long, was at the west end and destined to become the library. Moving toward the east was the dining-seating area with enormous windows facing the cliff. Then came the compact kitchen with very deep stone counters. A short hallway opened to the fishing room on the north and the front entry to the south and the two-vehicle garage at the end.

Upstairs at the west end was the master bedroom with a fine view of the cliff face, a bath with the deep Japanese soaking tub and a tatami mat exercise area and a walk-in closet. Between the master suite and the guest room and its bath at the east end was a large family room—the upstairs living room. I had asked for a mouse-proof attic and there were two, one at each end of the house, both marvelous, both finished rooms fitted with electrical outlets and good lighting. The small attic off the master bedroom I used for suitcases and travel gear. The large attic was lined with metal shelving to hold books and papers which multiply like summer gnats in a writer's house.

I met E, the young, intense project manager from Harry's office who seemed brimming with ideas, and felt I could depend on him for solving the inevitable problems while I was traveling out of the country. We began an e-mail correspondence concerning details of the plan.

Most of the experienced local house construction workers were making big money in the gas fields. One contractor didn't return my call for weeks and when he did it was too late. Another contractor who had done some work for me in Centennial said he was interested, but before things got serious he said he and his wife were getting a divorce and he was leaving Wyoming to start a new life. A local fellow—I'll call him Mr. Construct—looked promising and Harry and I had several meetings with him. He seemed willing and interested and I liked him as a person. Yet in some way I was uneasy about him and I did not think he grasped what I wanted the house to be. Perhaps it was the John Wayne poster on his office wall. Perhaps it was his office walls themselves, plastic-coated wallboard, probably left over from some other construction project. I felt he was a good, reliable builder, comfortable with standard housing and standard materials, but probably not particularly imaginative. What would he think about incorporating rusted metal and found objects into the house? I felt this house needed someone a little freaky, open to new ideas, an experimenter. Yet given the shortage of experienced labor, we might have to work with Mr. Construct.

Harry supplied him with plans and we waited for some kind of cost estimate. For many weeks there was silence. I had a tight budget. I also had a time budget as I was not getting any younger. I wanted to be in the house and on the property watching falcons and eagles. He did let us know that there was no way he could undertake to start the building until autumn. And that was a blow.

The year was wearing on. I drove over to the site as often as I could and tried to imagine the house. Late summer came and we still didn't have a builder. I was intensely conscious of fleeting time. The thick green smell of June had blown away in the western wind and now, in August, the grasses were curing out, scenting the wind with the slightly sad odor of hay. The pronghorn were in rut, plant seeds ripe and packed with nutrition. Wildlife was approaching its annual prime condition. Unlike modern humans who eat well every day despite seasons and weather, wild creatures undergo annual fluctuations in their physical condition—well-nourished and strong at the end of summer, weak and trembling at the end of winter, year after year on the seesaw of life and death. Summer stops suddenly in Wyoming. A cold snap or a beginner snowstorm hits for a day or two in August or early September, then relents for a last-chance golden autumn period of a few weeks. Then things get serious, the storms longer and more intense and the snow stays on the ground.

The property included a handsome little island, a shady cottonwood bosque, in the North Platte. Walking around on the island that August I found seven eagle primaries. (Primaries are the big outermost wing feathers.) For a few seconds I wondered if it had been a molt. But of course eagles do not molt bunches of feathers at once, but one at a time, and a loss of seven feathers would be catastrophic to flight. My Centennial friend, Uphill Bob, a walking encyclopedia of outdoor lore, but ever the optimist, said he thought this was not necessarily a sign of eagle demise (I had guessed someone passing in a boat took a shot at one). Yet when I asked the Yellowstone bird management biologist, Terry McEneaney, he said flatly, "That's a dead eagle."

One important chore that I could get going while we worked out the practicalities of construction was fencing out the neighbors' cows so the overgrazed and trampled land could begin to recover. Cows also eat young cottonwood trees, a habit which is gradually denuding the riparian margins of new tree growth, and their sharp hooves and heavy weights break down the riverbanks. I was surprised that The Nature Conservancy had allowed surrounding ranchers to run their stock on the property. Because we were beginning a conservation-restoration project I requested a clause be added to the conservation agreement excluding stock grazing from the property to protect it if it ever changed hands. The Nature Conservancy refused. Gradually I learned that this organization is allied with ranchers and is more concerned with land acquisition than conservation. Ranch owners often hold large acreages and it is a feather in The Nature Conservancy's hat to add big chunks of ground to their holdings, but they seem unconcerned with the actual condition of that land. They ignore the fact that heavy grazing severely damages plant diversity and, where there is water, stream banks and tree regeneration. It was also shocking to me that their habitat inspector failed to notice the noxious weeds—leafy spurge along the waterways, Canada thistle, cheatgrass and other troublesome invaders largely spread by cattle. I was completely disillusioned.

But first I needed a surveyor to run the lines. I was surprised to discover that the southeast property corner was actually in the river. If you buy coast or river property, as many people have discovered, you win some and you lose some. The county clerk recommended a fencer, call him Penn, a homesick refugee from Pennsylvania farm country whose father had come to Wyoming twenty years earlier, had seen a need for a fence business (ranchers and cowboys dislike this job) and stayed on. The Penns partially fenced the 520 acres at the top of the property, including the difficult steep run down the west end of the cliff. The fence was barbed wire with a bottom smooth wire and a sixteen-inch gap to allow pronghorn to get through. Pronghorn, unlike deer, prefer to crawl under a fence rather than leap over it. It was difficult for Mr. Penn to stay on the job. Always shorthanded, always struggling with broken equipment, always juggling other, more lucrative jobs, Mr. Penn had things on his mind. He told me one time that he had been in places on ranches where the owners had never set foot, and that once, pulling out a rotten old post, he had found a nineteenth-century Fort Collins whorehouse token, good for one night. Some long-gone cowboy had been disappointed when he got to town.

Near the house I preferred buck-and-pole fence to barbed wire and Mr. Penn put in a good-looking run along the river frontage. It was a little too close to the river and the next year, when the river rose higher than usual, it folded about six pole lengths of fence back upon itself. We didn't lose it, because my son Gillis made a web of ropes tying the folded fence sections to a stout cottonwood tree growing ten feet back from the river edge.

It got harder and harder to get Mr. Penn to continue fencing. After a year or so I tracked down another fencer, Charley, a big rangy guy from Nebraska who was strong and fast. He finished the barbed-wire fence on the south property line, replaced four hundred feet of bad old fence west of the house with new buck-and-pole, completely fenced the island with buck fence, fenced the far side of the river with more buck fence, repaired breaks, put panel curtains—sections of metal strips or large mesh that can be raised or lowered with turnbuckles according to the stream flow—across Jack Creek to prevent neighbor bulls from trespassing. In one long run along the east line at the top of the cliff acreage, he removed the flimsy electric-wire-topped fence and put in five strands of barbed wire after we saw the neighbor cows jumping high, wide and handsome over the electric. In all we put in six miles of fence because in addition to the perimeter of the property the riverbanks had to be protected. Neighbor ranchers' cows commonly left their own gnawed acres and used the shallow North Platte as the highway to better grass.

Another task that could be done early was putting in a new well. The original well was hundreds of yards distant from the house site and the water in it was powerfully alkaline, a local problem. Alkaline water tastes dreadful and was the scourge of covered wagon parties crossing Wyoming for neither men nor beasts could drink it for fear of blistering their tonsils and suffering agonizing stomach cramps. The Stolns were the expert local well-drilling team, a sibling group with a small farm in the middle of town—pond, cattails and ducks. In rural Wyoming family partners run many of the small businesses. At the Stolns' home place there was an acre or two of spare parts for every kind of machinery invented since the industrial revolution. Ms. Stolns kept chickens and sold eggs. The brothers drilled quickly and struck water almost at once. Of course, near the river the water table is not far away. The water was alkaline and just barely drinkable. We would have to find a water purification outfit.

I wanted to somehow ameliorate the wind and start landscaping the rough prairie. Tree and shrub windbreaks seemed the practical way and I engaged the landscape team, Deryl James and Dave Quitter of Trees Unlimited. They had rescued some of the botched landscaping at the Centennial house, and, as they lived in Saratoga, it was logical to get their help. I enjoyed several good talks with Deryl about landscaping, rocks and native plants. In the spring my son Gillis and I, following some arcane directions from someone who didn't really know, had tried to find a sage grouse dance ground—called a "lek"—northeast of Laramie. We did not find the lek but discovered some beautiful natural outcrops of rock and juniper, and raced from one to the next, proclaiming each rock-and-tree arrangement more handsome than the last. I took photographs to show Deryl who, when he saw them, said coolly that such groupings just happened to be his specialty. He and Dave and Deryl's younger brother Gerald began to put in striking assemblages of native trees and shrubs and rocks.

Only gradually did I realize that Deryl was something of a landscape genius who could have achieved fame and fortune in the wider world had he chosen. More revelations followed. His partner, Dave, was an experienced geologist who had attended the Colorado School of Mines and worked all over the world, specializing in precious gems and minerals. He also had a gift for keeping up with and understanding technology. Counting Gerald, the duo was actually a triumvirate, and that metamorphosed into a quartet when I learned that another brother, Dennis, lived in Alaska. As all but one of the men were brothers with the last name of James, it was easy to call them the James Gang, although Trees Unlimited was their professional name and they referred to themselves as "Trees." But the James Gang stuck as a moniker. Deryl said, in his serious voice, "Oh yes, and then there's our other brother, Jesse. He's somewhat estranged from the family." I am still waiting to meet Jesse. And the James Gang turned out to be much, much more than brilliant landscapers.

One day there came an e-mail from E. It said that he was leaving Harry's office to work on his own house. Harry made light of it but I was poleaxed. It seemed a very bad thing. In that moment I felt like one of P. G. Wodehouse's characters who, when things take a turn for the worse, sense that the iron has entered his soul. I believed then that I should halt the entire proceeding and sell the property. I made out a painful little pro and con list.

PRO

- The architectural design is almost finished.
- Harry T has more than a year of work already in on the project.

- I already have a lot of money in the place.
- Three miles of fence to keep cows away is up and paid for.
- The new well is in.
- Electric line is in and paid for.
- Doug, the furniture designer, has already started on the kitchen cabinets and shouldn't be stopped.
- The property will be more valuable with a house on it.

CON

- I'm afraid I don't have enough money for the whole enchilada.
- Cow trespass is an ongoing and difficult problem.
- We need three more miles of fence.
- The place is hard to get to and far from services and stores.
- There is a construction labor shortage thanks to the gas fields.
- Contractor can't start until late in the year.

The arguments were not evenly matched, and I thought it all over when I went up to our house in Gunners Cove, Newfoundland. Although I had cold feet, when my accountant remarked that the property would be worth more with a house on it, I decided to keep on chasing the dream.

It was a summer of back and forth between Centennial and Saratoga with easement papers, permits, right-of-way documents, then, in August, the long trip to Newfoundland and a decision to sell the old house there that I had spent more than a decade renovating. The travel to the Great Northern Peninsula was arduous and tiresome, the visit too short, as always. I chopped wood, peeled bark off the logs on the boat slipway, freed the ax from a clenched junk of wood and hiked the Raven

Trail. The house was in the Atlantic boreal region where the salinity of the open sea was around 35 percent, but inshore a little less from freshwater streams and rivers. In the tidal pools east of our wharf there was black whip weed, unknown this far north before 1928 (another proof of climate change?), laver, rockweed with its paired air bladders, northern rock barnacles, acorn barnacles, minuscule snails best appreciated under a magnifying glass, tiny reddish worms. In slightly deeper water were millions of blue mussels and green sea urchins, one or two purple starfish, a few moon and purple jellyfish. The year before there had been many jellyfish, but this year only a few.

One of the hard tasks was going through the fisherman's odds and ends from an earlier time that we had collected from the decrepit fish house before we tore it down, storing them in a box in the new boathouse. There was a fisherman's wooden lunch box with a string and nail to close it, a galvanized can for kerosene, a wooden twine reel for winding net line, a wooden piece with six holes bored in it to keep sled dog harness from tangling, several reels for cod or squid jigging, mallets for pounding in boat caulking, an animal hide stretcher, a fish knife, a barrel-hoop forcing tool, assorted hooks, a mold for lead fish-shaped sinkers, various whittled wedges and stoppers. I still sometimes think I can go back there and see these things.

I would miss the birds: a pair of furious peregrine falcons, a northern goshawk with a nest at the top of a deformed spruce leaning over the water, the three crow pals that worked the rockweed at low tide eviscerating sea urchins, then picked ripe berries on the hillside for dessert. One had a white spot on his neck. Piping plovers, difficult to identify gulls (which were herrings? glaucous? great black-backed?) and arctic terns were always there.

A final regret came when the nearby restaurant removed

turbot cheeks from their menu, a serious blow, as I thought this delicacy a prime reason to come to the peninsula. Never before or since have I discovered this dish in any restaurant or fish market. God knows where all the turbot cheeks of yesteryear have gone—probably home to the fisherman's missus.

Back in Wyoming, Harry Teague drove up to Bird Cloud with Jim Petrie, his new project manager. We all met in Mr. Construct's office, Harry looking slightly rumpled, grumbled about another speeding ticket on the Baggs Road—his second. He remarked that the state ought to put up a roadside sign saying that stretch of highway was supported by Harry Teague Architects.

Harry and Jim had brought all sorts of materials, including curious interior facings such as leather brick sheets (!) and some shiny copper panels also stamped in a brick pattern that I thought were ghastly. Harry said the copper would be a good covering for the entry room ceiling once a patina had developed. Someone said the best way to achieve that patina was to lay the sheets all out on the ground and pee on them. There were no volunteers. I disliked the shiny copper but said I would trust Harry on this one. Why do we hire architects? Why not sit down with a builder, as so many do, and work out what is wanted versus what can be done within a specific budget? Because, sitting down with the builder and listing what one wants, imposing one's choice of materials on the design, supports the human tendency to cling to what one knows rather than experiment. Part of what one pays an architect for is his or her experience and design sensibility and knowledge of unusual materials and new technologies. So I agreed to the copper brick sheathing, trusting the architect, and in the end it looked beautiful, a rich, dark patina with a subtle texture.

It was eight months since we had bought the property and

still we did not have an estimate of cost from Mr. Construct. I was conscious of arrows of weeks whipping past. And then, in late summer of 2004, Mr. Construct, after delivering a shocking estimate more than twice my budget and twice the local per-square-foot costs, said he could not undertake construction work for many months. Even then the rush of time was more important to me than the money. I reluctantly decided he could not build the house. What to do? I began now to meet with different so-called upscale builders in Laramie, but found their very expensive houses badly built and run-of-the-mill suburban schlock. Costs would escalate because the travel time from Laramie to the Bird Cloud site was more than two hours each way in summer. The workers would have to stay in local motels—and I would have to pay for all of it one way or another.

One of my three sons resisted the lure of the rock and the river and said he didn't really like the place. Another son advised me to wait at least a year before building. The third son and my daughter thought I should go ahead. Someone said just build a little cabin on the property and do the big house later. But a cabin couldn't hold all my books, never mind a bed, table and chair. Because I really wanted to live in this house, I decided to press on. I had no idea of the problems and hassle that would come with the house, all slowly building into stress, high blood pressure and frequent thoughts of fleeing to a tent in the dying forest. Years later I still wonder if I should have cut my losses and looked elsewhere for a house site.

But I didn't do it. The place was so beautiful, the great slab of cliff so vivid with birdlife, the plants and weeds so intriguing because unfamiliar, the rare *Penstemon gibbensii* still to be located, the night sky so full of constellations and meteors that even satellites, long-distance jets and the orange horizon glow from Saratoga's 1970s mercury vapor lights could be ignored.

The site of the future house at the north end of a valley bordered by the Sierra Madre and the Medicine Bow made me think of the explorer H. W. Tilman's description of Kashgar, situated in "a valley in which men might live a hard life and yet exult in living."[1] The river at sunset became mottled green and peach in patterns that recalled the marbled end pages of old books. Quickly the evening dusk filled with darting swallows, their dark bodies gradually absorbed by the intensifying gloom. The great horned owl called from the island and everything fell silent except the murmuring river and a more distant owl. In this place there was so much to know. I told myself the house had to be built. I began to think of it then as a kind of wooden poem.

I have difficulties with poetry, especially at the new-book bookstore, standing in front of the poetry shelves. I don't know what is wrong but I can never find what I know must be there. It is very different in front of the poetry shelves of the secondhand bookshop where every other worn volume promises pleasure.

I stumble into and around poetry, frequently knocked sidewise. Sometimes I don't know what poetry is, and it seems as plentiful as sagebrush on the steppes, and other times it seems that no poem has yet been written, just images and a few joined words flaring in some people's minds. What of David Nash's wildwood sculptures, are they not poems? And I suppose that a kind of animal poetry illuminates the Clark's nutcracker jamming yet another pine seed into its mouth. Bird Cloud was to be a kind of poem if a house can be that. After Bird Cloud was finished I knew it was a poem of landscape, architecture and fine craftsmanship when one of those yellow thunderstorms swept in near sunset with gold light spilling onto the ground

1. H. W. Tilman, *China to Chitral* (Cambridge University Press, 1951), 720.

and a rainbow. From the big windows I watched as the cliff went saffron as a candle flame, thunder marched around and hot lightning slammed the cliff. Pods of wind burst against the house with a side dish of chattering rain. In the east the towering bulk of the storm was a sulky purple-blue the shade of new denim, but in the west the sky was opening, showing a tender blue like the lining of an antique Chinese robe.

After a long day of reading bad outlaw "history," tiresome stuff on the greasy hijinks of western gunmen that strike so many westerners as the essence of the past, I took down Virginia Adair's *Ants on the Melon* (thinking briefly of the Gourds who, with a nod to V.A., made a song with the same name) and Alden Nowlan's *What Happened When He Went to the Store for Bread.*

I started with "Ants on the Melon," the poem, but instead, in my mind I kept hearing the voice of the Gourds' Kevin Russell, which always sounds to me like a graft of a carny hustler onto a Missouri River flatboat man, roaring about putting down his brown cow. It got between the lines and I swapped Ms. Adair for Alden Nowlan. Plainly I had been headed there all the time. I have loved Alden Nowlan from the dusty moment years ago in the slope-ceilinged upstairs room of a bookshop near the Bay of Fundy where I first opened this very book and read "Stoney Ridge Dance Hall," a poem I liked so much I almost fell over. A poem with homemade brass knuckles fashioned from bottle caps! I talked about Nowlan with the proprietor who loved "The Bull Moose." Now my favorite is not the brass-knuckled cousins, but the poem of his own beginning.

I'm in trouble, she said
to him. That was the first
time in history that anyone

had ever spoken of me.
It was 1932 when she
was just fourteen years old
and men like him
worked all day for
one stinking dollar.[2]

From the day of that reading I have loved this tender, fat, rural-poor poet who died too soon, unfinished. He had the Thing Which Cannot Be Explained.

The year 2004 was a year of travel and worry. It seemed that every few weeks I was making the long drive to Denver International, flying east in late afternoon over the tight irrigation circles below, over the veined watercourses in the hills, the dull purple and brown land flattening and dark. The first farmhouse light shone—someone in a house already built—and soon after the main street of a town fired up pinpoint streetlamps and gradually there emerged from the darkness rosettes and bouquets of light that were towns and in between solitary flecks indicating yard lights at some agricultural outpost. Finally the cities of the east floated up from the rim of the earth as electrified jellyfish.

And my own Thing Which Cannot Be Explained was how an entire year went by after we bought the Bird Cloud property with only three miles of fence, a half-mile power line and a well of alkaline water to show for it. I was slow to learn that delays and long waits are part of building.

2. Alden Nowlan, "It's Good to Be Here," in *What Happened When He Went to the Store for Bread* (Minneapolis: The Thousands Press, 1993, 2000), 128.

CHAPTER 5

The James Gang

Red
"barn dancer"
by Doug Ricketts

2004–2005

The year 2004 rolled on like a river stone traveling with the current despite my frustration at not having a builder's commitment, or an idea of cost. Everything seemed to be floating and I was on the road constantly, driving over to Saratoga to meet with Deryl James and Dave Quitter or to the county seat for one permit or another, or to Fort Collins, Colorado, for vehicle maintenance, or to Denver to visit the dentists. I have terrible teeth and much of my time and money goes into desperate hours getting implants and associated fixes. I am the perennial patient of several expensive dental experts. What is the collective noun for dentists? A crown of dentists? Or a brace of dentists? A pain of dentists is more fitting. There were many long days spent driving tensely to Denver, then back with throbbing jaws. And because I was working on a book about the Red Desert, there were camping trips into the Haystacks, to old Sulfur Springs, to Butch Cassidy's cabin, to Adobe Town, to Maggie Baggs's Nipple, to the Boar's Tusk, to many unnamed places, including the turnoff where grew several yellow prince's plumes (*Stanleya pinnata,* a member of the mustard family), indicators of selenium in the soil, a few miles beyond a favorite hillside packed with hundreds of fossilized stromatolites. And on the slope behind the prince's plumes, dramatically bisected by a fault, I found a tiny fossil trilobite.

The Red Desert is considered by most Wyoming people to be a six-thousand-square-mile chunk of empty and almost worthless public land. The area actually belongs to private individuals, the state of Wyoming and the Bureau of Land Management. Immigrants trekking to Oregon despised and feared it as a waterless desert, but nineteenth-century sheepherders from California discovered it was a good place to over-winter. Sheep fattened on the nutritious saltbush and found enough water. In recent years extensive oil and gas exploration and increased cow grazing have changed the ecology of this once-wild place. Less than 1 percent of the area is managed for wildlife habitat protection. Where early travelers saw sharp-tailed grouse, bison, bighorn sheep, grizzly bears, numerous beaver and even wolverines, today they see dust, feral horses, and noxious weeds including cheatgrass, halogeton and Russian thistle.

In 2004 I made two trips to Yellowstone for classes on waterfowl identification and raptors. Although it was only mid-September when the raptor class came up I couldn't get into the park through Beartooth Pass at the northeast entrance—it was already snowed in. Too bad. That was the best way into the park to reach the wildlife classes usually held at the old buffalo corral area in the Lamar Valley, and it avoided bear jams, those impassable dams of cars stopped anywhere so that the occupants could leap out and take wildlife photographs. The approach road ran through the stunningly beautiful Chief Joseph Highway and into wild Cooke City, a ragged town clamped onto the base of a steep peak, a snowmobile and ultrafreak town inhabited by proudly eccentric characters.

Living and traveling around the mountain states I learned the approximate days all the passes close and open. The pass separating Centennial and Saratoga in the Medicine Bow range was closed from late October until Memorial Day—seven or more long months. In summer the pass cut the trip to about fifty-five miles. On the winter routes it was more than a hundred miles. The worst road was I-80, a tussle with big trucks, black ice and high winds. The southern route down through Colorado on relatively empty but long and twisty roads seemed interminable. On this road I saw a strange accident; a cattle truck had somehow turned over and neighbor ranchers were rounding up the survivors. I could only think of the wretched cows swaying along in queasy, jolting half-light, then suddenly a lurch and a terrific violence as the world turned upside down.

On a very warm, golden October day Gillis came for a visit

and we went over the pass to check out the property. The place was ineffably beautiful, the cottonwoods a deep amber color. We walked around, drove to the east end in the bruiser SUV that I used for trips into the Red Desert, fished a little, sketched. We saw deer, a golden eagle, two bald eagles, two or three meadowlarks, an assortment of northern harriers. Gillis noticed the resident mink with a mouse in its jaws running along the bottom buck fence rail. In the distance we heard an avocet. As we were leaving, just before dusk, we noticed a large black porcupine in a cottonwood a few feet away from the fire ring. "It may have designs on Deryl's trees. It's good they're fenced," I said. Each tree stood within a circle of sheep fence to keep deer from browsing it. I didn't think porcupines could get through, but I soon found out they slipped in like greased eels and were serious tree killers. That was the last trip of 2004 to Bird Cloud. Gillis headed back to Santa Fe and I settled down for the winter in Centennial. I only made one or two trips to Bird Cloud over the next six months.

In January of 2005 I was invited to attend the Game and Fish wildlife biologist Ron Lockwood's elk-collaring project near Fossil Butte. The project was intended to help the Game and Fish Department learn specific information about elk populations and their whereabouts to answer claims by gas exploration companies that no elk were in such-and-such an area and therefore drill permits should be granted. The collar project would show how many elk went where.

The trap was a circular walled structure. The elk had been lulled into a false sense of security as the outer trapdoors were left open for months, the ground strewn with the finest alfalfa. After days of suspicious sniffing and circling the elk began to edge in at night, found they were out of the wind, discovered the nutritious hay. By January they were casually sauntering in, the shelter and the hay taken for granted, no doubt provided by some beneficent elk spirit. Then one morning before daylight while they were gobbling hay, Ron and his son Sam closed the outer doors, imprisoning the elk.

The night I arrived it was very cold, almost twenty below zero. In the morning Ron, still in his pajamas, stopped by my motel to make sure that I was up for the project and that my vehicle would start. My vehicle did not start and Ron said he would come back for me. He returned dressed in the heavy Carhartt coveralls ranchers wear on bitter days. Although Ron had a house and family, his truck was his real home. Bob, his Aussie heeler, usually sat in the passenger seat. The windshield sported a star fracture. An overhead rack carried two rifles, one with spotting scope. The rack had been installed in a hurry and there was no dome light. On the dashboard were two elk spike horns, a length of wire, a dirty white cowboy hat, a mesh Game and Fish cap, three pairs of gloves, a radio, various envelopes and forms, a calendar for the wrong month, an assortment of bumper stickers (SAVE THE RED DESERT: 50,000 ANTELOPE CAN'T BE WRONG, WAGE PEACE, LIFE IS GOOD, CRACK KILLS). In and around the front seat were hanks of baling twine and many pieces of clothing suitable for trips to Antarctica or Death Valley. We went to the Fossil Butte museum where Ron's team waited. As we left the warm museum a pygmy rabbit sprang from under a clump of rabbitbrush.

"Looks like snow," someone said in a joking tone.

We headed to the elk-filled corral. At the south end of this corral there was a closed-off smaller corral with equally high walls, and beyond it a long compartmented chute that could accommodate four animals. Inside the main corral Ron and Sam worked the elk one by one into the second corral and from there, pressed each one into the chute. The elk were furious and frightened. The team members stood along the sides of the chute compartments, each exhalation of elk and humans sending plumes of steam into the bitter air. The wind began to rise and bare fingers went numb in seconds. It started snowing. Hard. The air shuddered with volant snow like bead curtains in an earthquake. One person drew blood samples, another put the vials in a case, another put in left and right ear tags, checked teeth, another measured the neck, someone noted the data on a clipboard, another put an electronic collar on the unwilling elk, and two burly guys at the end of the chute opened a door and let the now thoroughly terrified elk out. The animals sprang away with prodigious leaps, plunging through deep drifts in a spray of snow and ice particles. In the whiteout the world fell away until there was nothing but panting elk and purple-faced humans. It was intensely cold, the snow thickened and the wind roared. It hurt to talk. After three or four hours it was over. One female elk, too frantic with fear to bear the experience, had tried to leap over the fifteen-foot trap wall and broken her leg. Her life ended there, a victim of human science. Ron gave me two elk antlers and they, supplemented with others from a Texas elk preserve, became the handles on Bird Cloud's cabinets. I thought antlers had to be the world's original handles; they were handsome, fit the human hand very well and were more comfortable to use than any wood, plastic or metal handle yet invented. Prehistoric Indian knives were sometimes hafted with antler. A few days after the elk roundup I was in New York where the only corrals were at street corners, waiting for the light to change.

The winter of 2004 through 2005 was good for cross-country skiing in the Medicine Bow range and I went out every day I could manage it, snowstorms or not, for the frigid day at the elk corral had made anything short of a blizzard seem petty. But people do have accidents in the forest, especially people who go out alone as I always did. One summer, walking on a marked trail I was startled to hear gunfire and the smack of a bullet into a nearby tree. At the bottom of the trail a carload of yahoos with Nebraska plates peeled out. And on a glittering Christmas Day a man on a snowmobile drove over a snow-covered stream. He went through the snow and ice and into the water where his machine died. Wet and on foot he quickly lost his ability to think rationally, blundering on through the drifts, confused and terribly cold. Eventually he reached the strange stage in the process of freezing to death when the body feels hot and confined and in one of his final acts he tore off his clothes. His naked corpse started a rumor that he had been found by thieves, robbed and stripped of his garments.

As the spring of 2005 advanced, the snow slumped in the growing hours of sunlight, softening the top layer. During the night the temperature dropped below freezing and the good snow was imprisoned beneath a hard casing of ice, impossible to ski. Only in the deep forest where the sun's melting rays could not ruin it did the snow stay loose. The Shiras moose shook their antlers in the willows. Rabbit and hare tracks were everywhere, as were the ancient signs of the changing season. In a few months the pass would reopen. In the meantime I went again to New York, back to Wyoming and then down to Taos and a few days later away to New York once more. In Taos I stopped at Garcia's fine tile shop south of town and bought a Mexican talavera sink for Bird Cloud's future downstairs powder room.

Once the pass opened and the roads dried it was time for

camping trips into the Red Desert. I had one more visit to New York in May, but the problem of Bird Cloud loomed. We still did not have a builder.

I was bemoaning that fact to a Saratoga friend who gave me a strange look and said, "You know Gerald James, don't you?"

"Of course. He helps Deryl and Dave with the landscaping."

My friend snorted. "He's the best damn builder in Carbon County, maybe in the state."

"Gerald? Gerald is a builder?"

"Yeah, but he's picky. He won't take on just any job. But if you can get him he's the best. Deryl and Dave work with him."

That night I wrote a letter to Deryl, whom I knew better than Gerald, asking if the trio would consider the construction of Bird Cloud. There were a few days of silence and I imagined Gerald refusing anything short of a Taj Mahal replica or pleading other work. But they said yes, setting aside their own plans to work that year building a snowmobile lodge on the Continental Divide where they owned property.

Doug Ricketts, a friend and notable furniture designer in the Texas Panhandle, agreed to work with Harry and Gerald and make the kitchen cabinets and metalwork range hood. The stone countertops would come from Laramie, from a business owned by the wife of the real estate agent who handled the sale of Bird Cloud. Wyoming was that kind of place.

On July 25, Gerald and I signed a contract for the James Gang to build Bird Cloud. Gerald would have preferred just to shake hands, an old western bond of trust that has pretty much disappeared, but I do not lead a handshake life as my obligations and fealties to heirs, publisher, extended family are many and complex. I began to learn that Gerald was determinedly cheerful and sunny, extremely detail-oriented, a workaholic, a stickler for high-quality construction, incapable of cutting corners, the kind of person who lies awake at night fretting over imperfections, then rises in the dark and sets the difficulty right. The youngest of the brothers, he is extremely thin, has shoulder-length blond hair and resembles a remnant hippie or Russian ice skater. He liked to pretend he was still twenty-five years old and his agility and fearlessness supported the statement. Both he and Deryl were smokers who could not stop.

Events quickly went into high gear. Josh and Jason of Western Water Consulting came and established the hundred-year floodplain bench. Land along rivers is usually characterized by floodplain levels related to past submergence in times of high water. New construction is supposedly regulated by federal, state and local rules. The hundred-year flood level is the marker for construction permits. But of course, things can go awry. Just ask anyone from New Orleans. And in 2010 we had a hundred-year flood. The house stayed high and dry, but the river took many sections of buck fence.

Deryl and I went to Rawlins, the county seat, to plead the case before the Carbon County Planning Commission for a rezoning of the property which had been listed as agricultural land for more than a hundred years. It was approved and rezoned as agricultural-residential, in keeping with the slow but steady trend of protecting the river frontage from housing and business developments. Heavy grazing and cattle on the riverbanks had damaged the ecosystem over the years. From the time we bought the property we had had trouble with trespass cattle, especially one ranch's red mountain-loving French Salers who made a steep path up the west end of the cliff to get to the nutritious sedge on top, and who waded up and down the river, climbing onto neighboring sections wherever grass and browse looked good to them.

In July the Gang moved their trailer south of the house construction site. On the phone Deryl said they would start construction the first Monday in August. At last.

Architect Harry Teague, who likes old metal as much as I do, designed the front and back entryways to be covered in rusted corrugated "tin." The search was on for a source. Harry teased us with photographs of an old building in a Colorado town covered with the stuff. The James Gang found something closer to home, barn siding on a local ranch, and they spent some days taking down the old rusted metal and stockpiling it at Gerald's shop.

Deryl convinced me that I would save a lot of money if I bought the Gang a secondhand Bobcat skid steer rather than paying to rent one. There just happened to be one for sale up in Casper, he said. I did buy it and Deryl immediately christened it "the puppy." With it the James Gang dug the hole for the foundation, evened out, scraped and prepared the site for the slab, dug the septic tank hole and lines, dug trenches for water lines, made and repaired road and driveway. The week after we signed the contract I had to go to Newfoundland for a week.

While I was gone, Gerald, who had been going through the plans carefully, noted "utility room not large enough." That is, not large enough for everything that had to fit into it. Two days later Harry and his project manager, Jim Petrie, came up from Aspen to mark the precise outline of the house on the ground for the slab and the location of the utilities which would need drains and electrical outlets. That was the moment to have changed the plans enough so that the mechanical room could be enlarged and have its own detached slab. Gerald reportedly brought the subject up in a quiet voice, but the plans stayed the same.

For the slab, no one would do except Catfish, a Saratoga concrete expert with standards high enough to satisfy Gerald. Catfish was affable, sported 1970s-style curly sideburns, looked to be around forty. His assistant was Jake in a red shirt that could be seen a mile distant. Thirteen loads of gravel came in for the subfoundation pad and twenty loads for the driveway and new entrance road Deryl wanted to put in. After weather delays, there was another delay because Catfish's current client's half-basement job suddenly changed to a full-basement job, and then there was a hole in the Rawlins prison wall that had to be repaired immediately. The final stage of my pour was the library at the west end. When I got there Catfish was power-troweling the still-damp concrete and Jake was taking down the forms on the earlier sections which were hard and flat, flaring off light like a grey lake. Now it was possible to see the real shape of the house with its odd inlets and archipelagos, possible to get a sense of the interior space. It was a great moment. The house was really going to be built.

The work on the foundation continued for six weeks, fussy and exacting. Catfish signed his name with a flourish on the first slab. The second slab was going to be the underlay for the concrete floor. I resisted Jim's siren songs about the beauty of concrete countertops in the kitchen. Yes, they could be stained any color and would be ground to a satin-smooth surface and so forth, but in fact they need more care than stone counters, and making them is tricky. When one is slopping olive oil and sauces around, worries about the countertop are a distraction.

The mechanical room size marked the beginning of an ongoing tension between Gerald James and Harry Teague. Harry would not give an inch on enlarging the mechanical room. "You'll have to work with it," he told Gerald whose native inclination to avoid architects was rekindled. Gerald, the electrician and the plumber held bitter meetings to solve the problem; the many pumps, tanks, gauges and furnace, wiring and pipes as well as the communications equipment simply could not fit into the tiny space allocated for that room. They worked out a two-level solution, the addition of a second-level steel floor able to carry great weight. It worked, but the room was and is very cramped. When anything went wrong and needed maintenance, this little room was a hot, tiny, noisy hellhole. Even with the second-level solution the big three-hundred-gallon incoming water tank could not fit in and it sits today in the garage, between the two vehicle-entry doors. I believe disregard for the mechanical room was one of Harry's rare blind spots, and we all smiled when we heard later that he had completely forgotten to include any mechanical room at all in his own firm's new building—everything had to be wiggled in under the stairs in a kind of afterthought emergency placement. I have since noticed that many architects loathe thinking about mechanical rooms, and so those crowded and catchall places frequently resemble the labs of mad scientists in old films.

I was back in Centennial working on the Red Desert book. At the Bird Cloud site materials poured in. Piles of thick-cut spruce for the siding sat in the sun to season. There were mysterious heaps covered with tarps everywhere. When the appliances arrived they were stored in Gerald's snowmobile trailer which sat pensively to one side. A well pump and pipe and a pump start box, special floor plugs meant to close around cords and wires arrived, tape for joints, a nail gun and coils of wire, lengths of pipe. The place looked like the construction site for a massive resort.

At the end of August 2005 we all took a break and went camping in a special corner of the Red Desert with the archae-

ologists Dudley Gardner and Russ Tanner. We had a grand time
exploring. The area had ancient charcoal drawings of horses
on the undersides of overhanging ledges. We followed a collapsed cut-and-bent juniper fence constructed in a technique
that vaguely resembled the laid and woven Midland hedges of
England. This mystery fence of seven miles perimeter enclosed
a large watered meadow. It was not clear who built it and for
what purpose. Was it an Indian game enclosure, a nineteenth-
century sheep rancher's work, or a sheep-counting enclosure
of the U.S. Forest Service which, from 1905 onward, tried to
regulate sheep grazing in the nearby national forest? We found
a photograph in the 1977 Wyoming Geological Association
field conference publication showing a line-drive fence in the
Absarokas that closely resembles this mystery fence.[1] There
may have been multiple uses over the years as successive waves
of people controlled the country, from Indians to white sheep
and cattle ranchers to Forest Service employees. Because the
Red Desert is so arid, objects last for a long time.

In August, after the hay was cut, the swells of land, especially
at dusk, seemed covered with chestnut velvet. Thousands of
years of running water have cut the land into V-shaped arroyos
and gullies that deepen into clefts. At setting sun hours those
V shapes filled with a gel of honey-colored light that changed
to burnt tangerine.

In September there was another glitch between builder and
architect. From the first conversations I had with Harry about
this house I had asked that solar panels be incorporated. Harry
Teague Architects gave the James Gang the name of a Colorado contractor to do the solar design and, noted Gerald, "at

1. Charles M. Love, "Geological Influences on Prehistoric Populations of
Western Wyoming," *Wyoming Geological Association Guidebook* (1977), 26.

least supervise installation." We called him Mr. Solar. Unfortunately the contact information failed to link the James Gang with him. The plumber and electrician, foaming at the mouth with frustration, needed the specifications to plan the wiring and plumbing. They finally discovered Mr. Solar was out of the country, in the Philippines. When Gerald complained to Teague Associates about the lack of information on the solar system he was told that they were not aware the solar design was expected from them. As recently as five years ago architects left solar design to the house owner and construction management. But a few years after Bird Cloud was finished, I was in a Santa Fe audience listening to a panel of architects discuss regional landscape and building design. Harry Teague was one of the speakers and I was delighted to hear him emphasize that the world was changing and that architects had a responsibility to be sensitive to new energy sources, materials and technologies such as solar. Still, back in 2005 Mr. Solar told Gerald that he hadn't done any design work, because he didn't know if the roof panel project was still on or not. Gerald assured him that the project was very much alive and the lack of plans was holding up construction. He requested proposal drawings, cost, terms, contract and Mr. Solar agreed to be on hand to oversee installation.

Haggling continued over the mechanical room's size and what had to be crunched into it. There was an animated discussion about why Mr. Solar insisted on two smaller water tanks instead of one larger tank. The plumber was losing his mind trying to design a system that would work for the complicated house. Plumbing and wiring diagrams were not part of the architectural design. A communications system was tricky. Because of the shocking cost of putting in a telephone landline we went with a satellite communications system and a wireless computer system. Jon Lang of Production Engineering in Fort Collins, Colorado, worked out the satellite Internet and computer outlets and layout as well as the house's sound system. The system was not fast, as signals were relayed from the ground to the satellite and back to the ground again, but it usually works except in adverse weather or during sunspot activity when the whole thing goes wonky or dead and nothing can be done except to unplug the connection box in the mechanical room, wait (occasionally for hours), plug it back in and hope— one of the drawbacks to living in the country.

In 2004 we had signed a lease with a neighboring rancher allowing her cows to graze the five hundred acres on top of the cliff for thirty days in September 2005. But a curious accident occurred. One of her cows somehow—why and how was the stuff of conjecture—tried to go through the eighteen-inch space between our last fence post and the edge of the cliff at the east end. The cow fell to her death and lay half in the river. The rancher felt it was my fault because Mr. Penn, our fencer, had left the tiny gap at the end of the fence; she quoted a four-figure value for the cow. I asked Mr. Penn to dangle in space and add a projecting extension to the fence so it couldn't happen again. A regrettable coolness between me and the rancher persists to the present. The only winner in this bovine tragedy was the resident mountain lion who watched the corpse and took an interest, perhaps proprietary. Somehow the cow floated down the river to our island where the lion dragged it onto the shore, likely getting a good dunking itself when it crossed the river. As the James Gang worked on the house they were treated to a view of the lion a few hundred yards away eating steak day after day. The next spring I found the cow skull in a depression near the house. There was no help for it: we renamed the site of the accident Falling Cow in homage to

Frank Lloyd Wright. The skeleton and pieces of sun-faded hide lay on the east end of the island for years. And I now suspect that the mountain lion may have deliberately driven the cow off the cliff, as it later drove a deer.

One thing I had really wanted in this house was a deep Japanese wooden soak tub. In my early twenties, married to a man in the Air Force, I had spent nearly two years in Japan and loved the deep wood and stone tubs of some of the mountain resorts. Immersed in hot water, leaning against the fragrant hinoki wood and watching clouds fly through the wintery blue sky above encouraged haiku thoughts. The house design included other Japanese elements, especially an exercise area adjacent to the tub and bathroom fitted with tatami mats and walled with sliding shoji panels.

My Centennial friend Bob Cook, a.k.a. Uphill Bob, had built a plank bridge about twenty feet long to the island. It was anchored to the world on the island side by a cable attached to a long spike. When high water came in June the rising current lifted the bridge up and deposited it neatly on the bank of the island. But when the water went down, the marooned bridge was extremely heavy and awkward to move back into place even with a winch and motorized hauling. In 2009, working with the advice of the Army Corps of Engineers, the James Gang replaced it with a ninety-foot-long bridge, and Bob's old bridge, moved downstream, became a boat dock.

Dave Quitter, an expert with all things pertaining to earth, water, air and fire, worked out a reverse osmosis system for the household water, freeing us from alkali deposits. Alkali causes upset stomachs and undrinkable coffee and leaves a white, crusty residue on walls, in sinks and tubs, in clothing and water pipes. In spring after the thaw, alkali flats glittering with white alkali salts blossom on the landscape.

Interspersed among the stages of frame construction came landslides of small problems—the color of window hardware, an affordable source for the doors—and decision confirmations seemed to hang fire because people were on vacation, not in or didn't return calls. Gerald counted materials over and over—flanges, metal bits, boards, panels, boxes of screws and nails and brackets, and every day he and the crew studied the plans and the many minute changes that could throw everything off if overlooked.

There were moments of relief. In late September of 2005 a dozen trespass cows trampling the riverbank at the far end of the property pulled everyone off the site for the Great Cow Chase. With shouts and yodels, crashing of willows, hurled stones and screeches we drove the cows out. Gerald's frustrations burned up like tissue paper. One cow, used to cowboys on horses, was so demoralized by humans chasing on foot that she leaped a five-strand barbed-wire fence like Nureyev and landed in a different neighbor's pasture at a full gallop, leaving the top strand of wire severely stretched.

At the end of every day the site was scrupulously cleaned—Gerald allowed no wood scraps or sawdust or dirty plastic or spilled nails or strewn tools. But scrupulous tidiness takes time and Gerald the perfectionist lost his chance to go elk hunting up north in Ten Sleep country.

October began warm, sunny and clear, though the year before at that time the Snowy Range Pass was closed. The James Gang pled for faster decisions on materials to take advantage of the good weather. Catfish hoped the good weather would hold until Thanksgiving so he could get caught up. I hoped that in the mountains at least it would snow hard and soon so skiing could begin, though I was willing to give up skiing for decent construction weather.

In mid-October the James Gang and I went down to see Dudley Gardner's archaeological dig south of La Junta, Colorado, in a place the Park Service calls the Picketwire Canyonlands, "picketwire" being the Anglo rendering of Purgatoire. On the way we stopped at the stone yard to choose the kitchen countertop material. We wandered through the stacks of stone, every polished slab more beautiful than the last, Dave the geologist giving a running description of the kind and source of each. I thought I wanted a dark green but then saw a slab of streakily wavering, striated peach and grey and umber that resembled ancient dry riverbeds seen from the air. That was The One. Dave said it was a migmatite granite at a transitional stage between metamorphic and igneous, formed when the deep rock was the consistency of toothpaste, which caused the swirling, sinuous banded effect. I got a sample to send to Doug Ricketts so he could think about colors, as I thought intense saturated stained cabinet doors would satisfy my longing for brilliant color—this attraction maybe something about coming from northern climes, maybe some residual Québec taste. I like a colorful, handily cluttered kitchen and Bird Cloud's cabinets and drawers in red, violet, aquamarine, burnt orange, cobalt, lime, brick, John Deere green and skipjack blue inspires stir-fries, osso buco, grilled prawns, Argentinean salads of butterhead lettuce, tomato, sweet onion, roast lamb with Greek cucumber and dill sauce, frittatas, rhubarb sauce with glasses of dry Riesling for the cook. You bet.

Walking along the drought-afflicted and shrunken Purgatoire River, we had an unusually good look at the longest documented dinosaur trackway in North America. Here over thirteen hundred footprints of the plant-eating apatosaurus (a.k.a. brontosaurus) and the carnivorous three-toed allosaurus, ripple marks, a few clams, a palm frond and some horsetails, fish bones, ooids have all solidified into solid rock. The tracks were made by animals trudging along the shoreline of a shallow, quiet lake many millions of years before humans evolved. What had the local Indians made of those tracks? Did they have nightmares? Did they work dinosaurs into their mythologies? The site was not well-protected and during the recent dry years a desperate rancher had illegally loosed his cows on it.

One afternoon Dudley showed us a wall of extraordinary rock art depicting a large variety of wild animals that seemed connected by a rope, though it may be a "spirit" rope. Nearby stood an immense high boulder fortified with sharp rocks all around the edge rather like a crenellated castle; the giant rock seemed to be someone's long-ago last stand, causing the same intense shivers as seeing Canyon de Chelly or Mesa Verde.

Near sunset we poked around the ghost town of Dolores with its penitente church, the ruined altar disconcertingly decked with fresh flowers. This so-called Mexican settlement dates back to the late nineteenth century. The ground between sagebrush shrubs was littered with sparkling bits of iridescent broken glass, chunks of Mama's best china, belt buckles (which seem to have great staying power), rusted cans. The sun-thickened sole of a shoe curled up and young tarantulas scampered through the vegetation. In the evening they roamed the area, their eyes shining in firelight or flashlight. We looked for the entrance holes of trap-door spiders which are common here, and watched for rattlesnakes which are also common.

The next day on the way home we detoured to Bent's Fort on the Arkansas River fifteen or twenty miles above the place where the Purgatoire joins the larger river. At the time the original building went up, the Arkansas was the dividing line between the United States and Mexico; Bent's Fort stood on the U.S. side of the border.

I love this fort. It is one of the National Park Service's triumphs, a national historic site, and one of the truly important places to visit for those interested in the history of the west. It was planned as an Indian trading post for the business partners Charles Bent and Ceran St. Vrain, and was tremendously important in opening the west, although it existed for only sixteen years before William Bent set fire to it in 1849 for complex reasons. The original adobe structure, like a walled castle to eastern eyes, was modeled after New Mexico *placitas,* large square adobe buildings with interior courtyards and defensive towers. The fort was finished in 1834. The central courtyard was as large as a town plaza. This huge open space contained a massive buffalo-hide press. Ranged around the hollow square there was a blacksmith shop, a gunsmith's workroom, carpenter shops, trade rooms, council rooms, dining rooms, private sleeping rooms, and, at the rear, a wagon room that could hold fifteen prairie schooners next to the cactus-girded corral. Upstairs, between the watch towers, was a promenade with a view of miles of country in all directions, and more rooms, including a billiard room. In its day there was also a kind of local zoo on the second floor with a caged eagle and other prairie wildlife. The ruins of the fort continued to be variously used until late in the nineteenth century as a stage stop, a cattle ranch, and a post office.

Bent's Fort was meticulously reconstructed in the 1970s after years of study and archaeological excavation. Many of the unearthed artifacts are now part of the exhibits. It gives the visitor direct contact with the past, Mexicans, the mountain men, trappers, Indian tribes, traders and travelers who used the fort, the wildlife and domestic animals which kept it vigorous. In its day it changed the lives of everyone who came near the place, influenced national policies, destroyed the past and offered a brass ring to whomever could catch it.

Back at Bird Cloud in late October there was a strange interlude with no wind, clouds moving overhead very slowly. I saw a pile of fence poles on the riverbank. Had the fence builder finally hauled them from the river where they had languished since the spring's flood? Or did the James Gang rescue them from the drink and stack them up for the fencer? The James Gang, of course. The stone patio Dave had constructed near the river was curved and shaped to fit the shade, but the picnic table that Uphill Bob had made and that we brought over from Centennial was uncomfortable. Will I ever know why he put the bench planks round side up? Very contrary.

Another chance to get something right came and went. Jim Petrie mailed Gerald the specs for the master bath. If I had practiced what the lawyers call "due diligence" and had gone over the plans with him, I might have ended up with the master bath I expected.

Although I wanted the same amount of storage space as in the Centennial bathroom, I had fallen for an architectural-home-design magazine photograph of a svelte sink with a background photograph of the ocean thundering onto a beach and asked if this sink could be part of the design. It could. So the fancy sink was ordered. But the desired storage space did not make it into the design. In the end the fancy sink was shoehorned between the shower and a window and there was no room to add storage space anywhere. Above the snooty sink hung a mirror with high-wattage bulbs blazing straight into one's face rather like something John Gielgud might have had in his dressing room. For an aging woman it was frightening rather than useful. The mirror was not the medicine chest type that opened to reveal shelves. It didn't open at all. We replaced it with a large, utilitarian medicine chest. At least now there was somewhere to keep all those little bottles and jars. Don't architects have these things in their bathrooms?

Walking near Jack Creek in the fading autumn light I noticed that the beaver of last year had not returned, washed out by the June flood although its dams were still partially there. About five ducks—too fast to identify, probably goldeneyes—were in the creek as I neared the bridge. Two deer ran east and six magpies sat on six fence posts. A cloud of gnats rose from the water. I heard a hawk's hoarse call but could not see the bird. The air was so calm that flying was probably laborious, and when a light breeze slipped in—not from the west but out of the east—a big redtail climbed up to play along the cliff face, then dropped down to skim low. On the way back I stopped where the top of an old cottonwood, broken off by lightning or wind, landed upside down, branches pronged deep into the soil. The bark was almost two inches thick and very deeply furrowed. What service does such thick, furrowed bark perform for the tree? In the river a huge trout leapt five feet out of the water. Was it chased by a bigger trout? Could there be a bigger trout? Or was it making an impossible try to snag the low-flying redtail?

It was a golden day of great silence, the wind quiet, the river a dark reflecting surface showing the buffy cliff. A large stone above the west end tower looked as though it might soon fall. All colors were pale yellow, faded ocher, dry-grass beige, pepper-seed white. There was snow high on the Sierra Madre around the source of Jack Creek. It wouldn't be long. As always I was overcome by the beauty of the place and by the turning of the great wheel of seasonal change.

On the first of November the forms came off the concrete.

Now the house had a floor, but the framing lumber was not on the job site. Dennis headed back to Alaska until the framing work was ready to start. On the fourth of November it snowed off and on all day and the next day was cold, but not too cold to backfill the foundation. Somewhere in those chilly days the James Gang put a combination lock on the front gate. They gave me the combination but when I drove from Centennial to the site the long way round and dialed the combination the lock would not open. I didn't realize one had to shove the lock hoops up into the works for the final click. I was not happy about the lock but supposed that the Gang was concerned about thievery, a problem with construction sites. The blame always falls on "kids" but there was at least one grown man in town who was observed at a party boldly stuffing an entire cold salmon under his jacket.

November kept sliding by. Gerald and Jim constantly discussed how post and sill plate had to come together, how to join the trusses and floor. The roof, the trusses, the beams all were tricky, load-bearing crucial parts that had to join perfectly. And Gerald needed the floor beams which were somewhere in transit. Suddenly everything stopped. Harry's roof engineer, J. Horne, decided that someone at the truss builders had miscalculated the load where the beams tied together. So now J. Horne and Jim were rethinking which beams must be used. Jim told Gerald that he would let him know the next day whether we could order and wait for the beams, or whether the beams were in Denver, or whether we had to have the beams manufactured. For once Gerald was upset but Jim, "my hero," said Gerald, resolved the floor problem and calmed the combatants. The floor package would be at the site on the second of December. The roof package still hung fire. Now the time had come to ask Doug Ricketts down in the Texas

Panhandle about his ideas for the kitchen and powder room cabinets.

I met Doug Ricketts in the late 1990s when I was doing research in the archives of the Panhandle-Plains Historical Museum in Canyon, Texas, for the novel *That Old Ace in the Hole*. I was interested in everything about the panhandle, and, as I often do, had fallen in love with the big cranky place. I was hungry to learn more. It was December and I came downstairs into the main hall of the museum to find everything in an uproar with people rushing back and forth, dragging boxes, moving tables and generally setting up booths and spaces for a Christmas fair sale. I took a quick walk through the exhibits although the event had not officially opened, seeing blown glass, ceramics, knitting, aprons, paintings of local landscapes, tree ornaments, bird carvings. Then, around one corner, I saw some wonderful furniture, elegant but sturdy, sensible but with a sense of humor and obviously made of old bits and pieces. I very much liked a dark green sideboard with a metal lattice-work on the doors. There was a tall cabinet with skinny legs and a round red metal top that looked like a young, redheaded dancer ready to clog—the piece was even called "barn dancer." The maker of this furniture was nowhere around, but I wanted to buy the sideboard. Finally the director of the fair found him and I met Doug, lanky and tall, mild, soft-spoken. I bought the sideboard and we managed to get it into the back of my truck. I was headed for Wyoming and it seemed sensible to get it while I had transportation. But it didn't stop there. I became friends with Doug and his newspaperwoman wife Kathy, both of them helpful in every way in showing me panhandle history and mores. Later their daughter Lindsay worked for me at Bird Cloud, helping put the bookshelves together, moving, sorting, cataloging and shelving my many books, doing research, keeping up with the office minutiae and giving me time to write. I was able to write the collection of stories *Fine Just the Way It Is* because Lindsay handled the day-to-day problems and did some research for me.

December arrived cold and snowy. From early morning until dark between the *chunk! chunk!* of nail guns and the scream of power drills Gerald was drenched in a waterfall of details of wall finishes, hinges, straps, colors, jambs, shoji panels, tatami mats and Polygal windows. The roof, truss and floor beam assembly was still not resolved as the truss company representative said she had not received okays from all the players. Apparently the roof engineer was the holdout. No one knew why. We all pictured him as a wizened, crotchety old man who enjoyed making life difficult for others.

The Warmboard was tentatively scheduled for delivery through the local lumber yard. Nothing in the construction world can be done directly between supplier and contractor; everything must go through a middleman which slows up the work and adds expense and another layer of bureaucratic confusion. Warmboard was to be the integral part of our radiant heating system. It would conduct heat from warm water in subfloor tubes to the floor surface—silent, efficient and even. The Warmboard itself also served as sub-flooring.

On Pearl Harbor Day, it was thirty below zero and clear; the floor package was delivered. The next day the James Gang came over to Centennial for dinner and I made decisions on the bathroom tile, grey stone, nixed knotty pine as trim or anything else, having a dislike of it as reminiscent of moldy New England motels going for the antique look. My father liked knotty pine which struck him as old Yankee. It was time to choose the wood for the upstairs floor and Gerald had brought along Jim Petrie's sample book. I thought that Alaskan yellow cedar, a rich golden color in the book, would be beautiful. I had bought some wrought-iron hinges in Santa Fe earlier expecting they could be used but Gerald said they would not work on house doors. They were better for outdoor gates. And although Catfish was a fine concrete worker he had not done a large colored and polished floor. At my request we would use Mr. A, a Fort Collins man, for the ground-level concrete floor. Two years before he had made a beautiful polished concrete floor in my oldest son's house and we expected a similar result.

Gerald and crew put up walls all through December in fluctuating weather. The tatami mats in the master bath area caused headaches in figuring the floor height, the set depth of the Japanese ofuro tub and the shower drop so that everything would come out level.

Although the cold snap let go and the weather warmed up, the roof engineer and the truss company were still not in agreement. Dave was trying to track down sources and prices for Alaskan yellow cedar to use in the upstairs floors, stair treads, trim, doors. The truss company was still waiting for the roof engineer "to send detail on section 3 where hip line hits trusses." The engineer apparently wanted to notch the cross-plied laminated veneer lumber (LVL) board to sit on the ledger board, but the truss company rep told Gerald that if he beveled the ledger board and added some bracketing to support, she would STAMP PLANS & BUILD. This was what Gerald had been waiting for and he said: "Don't notch LVL." But Jim Petrie agreed with the roof engineer about the notching. Gerald wrote, "I told him I'm going to do it [the truss company's] way. We'll see what I get away with." Snowy, blowy days halted the work and after the snow stopped, the Gang had to plow and sweep and shovel before the nail guns could bang again. On December 30 the stamped and approved trusses arrived.

A few days before Christmas Mr. Penn's helper ran over the septic system's inspection pipes. The Gang wasted the next day fixing the septic break and billed the fencer for it but waited two years to be paid. That's a typical country habit, too.

So ended 2005.

CHAPTER 6

When the Wind Blows

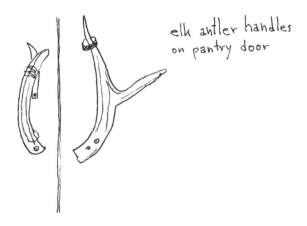

elk antler handles on pantry door

2006

When the wind blows in summer the entire landscape sways, grasses lean and twist, the willows thrash dementedly. In winter hurricane winds, loose snow loops sidewise in a grinding haze and the whole sky rolls like the ocean, hurling birds like rocks. At seventy, eighty, and one hundred miles an hour the winds pack concrete-hard drifts across the road. Feathers of snow curl off the top crests like the streamers off Everest. Only the cliff holds steady. It did not move through the winter of 2005–2006 though powerful gusts made it seem possible that great slabs of rock might shear off like icebergs from a calving glacier.

The framing continued through cold and windy January and

every few weeks the entire Gang went to the chiropractor—
"the bone bender"—to have their bodies realigned. Some days
were too cold for them to work. On my occasional visits to the
site I watched the skeleton of the house grow ever higher, a
bony structure like dinosaur bones against the cliff.

The invisible curmudgeon, Harry's roof engineer, called
to say he found the James Gang's detailed construction photographs on their Internet site extremely helpful, an innova-
tion in the construction world. The yellow cedar floor samples
were still to come and I was anxious to see them, but the weeks
passed and they did not arrive. By the end of January, Gerald
was thinking about the Polygal windows, a narrow row of blue
along the upper story that would make the house look like an
ocean liner. He planned to put some Polygals together to see
if the real dimensions matched the specs, suspecting the real
windows would be a quarter inch larger, a huge discrepancy in
his book. We were all thinking about the downstairs polished
concrete floor, and how great it would look.

Early in the design process Harry and I had talked about
shadow and sunlight. One of Harry's specialties is the play of
interesting luminosities. I very much like oddly shaped sliv-
ers of sunlight and moving shadows in a building, a kind of
architectural calendar in the way the Chaco Canyon ruins
indicate solstice and season. On the north side of the house
Harry designed a long, second-story metal pan to catch rain-
water and drain it away. After rain or snowmelt the reflection
of water in the pan shimmered on the upstairs ceiling like liquid moiré. The play of light throughout the house became an
ever-changing pleasure.

In mid-February Gerald worked on the roof of the fishing room entryway in twenty-below-zero weather. That old
enemy, the wind, rose and gusted to sixty miles an hour. The

wind kept coming. And in the hurricane days the yellow cedar samples arrived. I bucked a hundred miles of strong gusts on I-80 to see them. They were a disappointing muddy grey, very unlike the shining gold in Jim's sample book. We returned to Harry's original suggestion of recycled southern pine.

Brief runs of the painfully bright and cold Wyoming days that burn your eyes out of their sockets gave way within hours to new snowstorms. Heavy snow again stopped construction and brought back the sport of shoveling. Between storms Gerald and Dave worked on making the walls, hip roof, west window and metal pan.

A few good days turned into a midmonth blizzard, but then came an unprecedented run of eleven sunny, warm days. The county road was still a mess of drifted ruts and somehow Gerald cajoled the plow operator into clearing the road as far as our gate. The Gang did prodigious amounts of work in this warm interlude sweeping snow away, building walls, framing the metal pan and milling a big log from their private stock to use as a tie beam in the family room. They put the beam in place and wrapped it in brown paper.

In mid-April everyone associated with the house design and construction gathered to see what had been done. Uphill Bob and I drove over from Centennial. Doug Ricketts brought samples for the cabinet doors. We were all delighted by the bright stain colors, silky finish, metal of various shades and textures set in brilliantly stained wood frames, colors that complemented the variegated granite countertop. Rather than restrict the cabinets to one set of colors we decided on an assortment for a very high-colored kitchen. I loved the colors then and I love them now but they are not the prevailing market taste of bland monochrome cabinets featured in home *moderne* magazines. I thought I wanted a topaz- or ocher-colored floor, perhaps to echo the golden-grassed landscape, but Doug's cabinet door samples sat uneasily beside yellow hues. Harry suggested a terra-cotta red and he was right.

During the visit, as always, the site was spotless—no piles of rebar, no heaps of wood scraps, no mounds of dirt, no strew of nails and screws. Scrap wood went into a barrel as soon as it was made, the building was swept daily, all was remarkably tidy producing an atmosphere of control and calm, in marked contrast to the messy, noisy confusion of most building enterprises. The James Gang seemed to read each other's minds and operated in a Zen-like cloud of quiet concentration.

Harry and Jim liked what they saw. The construction was of high quality, every joint true and fair, the top of the house not an eighth of an inch off from the base. The window openings enclosed the magnificent views of the cliffs and the clerestory windows brought softened light. Everyone took turns climbing into the recess for the Japanese tub and imagining how it would be. The view from the tub recess was yellow cliff, gliding birds, wind-driven cloud.

Betty, Dennis's wife, who had worked hard carpentering since October, went back to Alaska and on the next day Deryl and I flew to Scottsdale for a visit to the Mayo Clinic. Deryl had some mysterious disease for which he had been given four or five different frightening diagnoses, depending on which Wyoming clinic or doctor he visited. Not knowing what was wrong must have been nerve-wracking. And I had a problem with my right hip and wondered if it was arthritis or worse. The advantage of going to the Mayo was that everything from tests to surgery could be done on-site; in Wyoming medical care involved a tremendous amount of driving with test centers scattered over hundreds of miles, bad weather often canceling appointments.

Deryl and I rented a red car in Scottsdale. The Phoenix-

Scottsdale area was difficult to reconnoiter, with endemic highway construction, and a tangle of similarly named streets, avenues and roads. The first evening we discovered a good place with a large tree-shaded patio for dinner and margaritas in Scottsdale's Old Town section. It was warm, with a slight breeze instead of a freezing Wyoming gale. Deryl was anxious, not wanting to hear what he thought he was going to hear.

I saw a doctor who said my hip problem was bursitis, which would likely respond to treatment and care. X-rays showed the joints were fine. Deryl discovered he did not have bone cancer with six months to live, but probably a problem with certain nerves; the medications he had been given up north were slowly killing him. He took a massive battery of tests over the next few days, including a visit to the Smoking Doctor, who did not harangue him about smoking but expressed calm disapproval. Deryl claimed many doctors have congratulated him on not smoking, and remarked that his lungs show no signs of deterioration.

As soon as we returned to Wyoming the weather worked itself up, buffeting the site with seventy-mile-an-hour winds. The weather bureau's definition of a hurricane wind is seventy-four miles per hour, but such violent weather is so common in Wyoming everyone just says "*really* windy" and lets it go at that. The next day it snowed too heavily for roof work and the Gang spent a warm day in Gerald's shop shaping tie beams and making the never-ending phone calls for shipping dates and materials inquiries.

The wind kept coming for the rest of the month, but the windows arrived and were roped to the walls awaiting installation. With the help of a rented boom truck and operator the beams for the family room went in place.

Gerald in particular, but all the James Gang, had a way with wild animals. Indeed, rabbits were more or less living in the still-open house. On the first day of May 2006 they (the Gang, not the rabbits) started putting plywood on the roof, a big job, dangerous when the wind picked up. I constantly worried that skinny Gerald would be carried miles away clinging to a sheet of plywood. They set a date for the wizened curmudgeon, J. Horne, to visit the site. Every day they shifted objects, trailers, piles of material to make room for incoming. The resident jackrabbits rolled their eyes seductively at Gerald and lay on their backs like cats.

Everything was blue board, sleepers, brackets, plywood and work on the pan. On the appointed day for the roof engineer's inspection visit, the sun was shining and the air balmy. We all expected a grouchy old bald head but he turned out to be young, magazine-model handsome, and very open and cooperative. He said all that he inspected was good. He even asked for constructive criticism and Gerald was pleased to show him "a better system of rafter soffit tails, that he can use on other sites." After these pleasant days the weather did a Wyoming thing and flared up, so hot that clouds were a relief. I headed for New York to talk about Jackson Pollock and the influence of the southwest Indians on some of his early work. When I got back the steel-clad exterior doors were in, very handsome and giving the house a feeling of solid strength that went well with its massive, sculptural personality.

I planned a trip to the Haystack Mountains in the Red Desert at the end of May and invited the James Gang to take a break and come along. The geologist Charles Ferguson came over and met the James Gang while we were packing for our camping trip. The photographer Marty Stupich was already out in the Red Desert and we would meet him at a prearranged place. Uphill Bob joined us.

We threaded the cat's cradle of roads and obscure tracks and reached the Haystacks around noon. We set up camp, then explored, looking for minerals and fossils before cooking dinner and building the campfire. A wild stallion showed up in an aggressive mood. He snorted a few times, then galloped away. Overnight the wind began to rise and by the next morning we could look south toward Colorado and see great plumes of dust bowling along the ground like desert djinns. There was an uneasy, ghost-ridden feel to the place. These dust devils were not uncommon in the desert, but had increased in number as gas energy drill rigs and work trucks broke up the cryptobiotic crust that holds the fine soil in place. We escaped from the wind by going down into a huge wash framed by sandstone towers topped with pink hats and continued to explore. The wash was packed with eroded caves, strange formations, pebbles and domes, gullies and pale walls. I saw a parent hawk carry a rabbit to its nest behind one of the towers.

When we came up out of the wash to make lunch, the wind was shrieking, stinging our eyes, ears, faces with dust. The wind was too strong to make sandwiches as it blew the bread away and hurled the hamburgers out of the pan, flung the pan down in the dirt. Marty called home and got a weather report that predicted snow and blizzard winds for our area that afternoon. We stuffed the tents in the vehicles—they could be folded later in a quieter place—then cut and ran. At home, brushing the grit and dust off my skin and out of my hair I decided to look at it under the pocket microscope my daughter-in-law Gail had given me for Christmas. I was amazed to see what looked like tiny pieces of glass. I mentioned this later in a talk to an outdoor group and an older man spoke up and said that he was a geologist and this dust looked like glass because in fact it was glass deposited by Yellowstone's last eruption over 600,000 years ago. That swung our thoughts to the rumor that Yellowstone was "overdue" for another big eruption that would wipe Wyoming and much more off the map. The geologist laughed and said we had another hundred thousand to a million years before it was time to worry. Television science is usually high comedy to professionals.

The day after our return from the Red Desert all was calm. Snowplows had opened the pass to Centennial saving fifty miles of driving in each direction. Time seemed to be galloping and I mentioned to the James Gang that it would be good if I had a move-in date as I had to get the Centennial house on the market soon. Gerald said that in a perfect world October 15, 2006, was the date, but in the real world December 15 was more likely. That gave them seven months to get it all done, and those seven months shot past like a squeezed bar of wet soap.

At Bird Cloud the summer went on for the James Gang in a chase after the right products. At this time we were thinking of alder for the baseboard and trim. I wondered how thin metal baseboard would look. Gerald went for the idea and experimented. When he brought a lengthy section in and laid it along the base of the wall we saw it harmonized perfectly with the character of the house.

The summer days were hot and punched through with brief showers. The plumber and the electrician were working hard. Gerald found something else to keep him awake at night. "Back door panty line 3/8" shorter than kitchen window & dining window. TRYING/FIGURE IT OUT." At this point I had written twenty-two hefty checks to the James Gang, and others to Harry Teague. While I worried about money Gerald sanded the roof edge and made it ready for trim and primed every inch of bare wood he could find. Steadily the metal roof went on as all metal roofs must—in the middle of a heat wave.

On July 4 we had something of a construction party at the river. My son Jon and his wife Gail came up and we grilled meat, drank wine (Mountain Dew for Gerald), ate lots of salads and vegetables (only meat for Gerald). The eagles watched. A few days later Uphill Bob and his sister Carol came over from Centennial to take a look at the place. Once again to the grill and the vino.

It was Dave's turn to visit the Mayo Clinic to see what could be done with his bad ankle, seriously smashed years before when their big tree spade turned over, taking him with it. Since then he'd walked awkwardly and in considerable pain, often pale and exhausted at day's end. He came back with the word that having the ankle fused would relieve him of a great deal of pain and make his walking gait closer to normal. On the Mayo's advice he made an appointment with one of Wyoming's excellent bone and joint doctors—fixing ranch-work and rodeo accidents makes these medicos tops in this field.

Mr. Solar installed the panels in stages, zooming back and forth between Colorado and Wyoming. The copper sheets for the two entryways and the upstairs family room ceilings arrived, ugly-shiny, though Gerald planned to age them to a pleasant patina. But where were the Polygal window frames? Two weeks in the future. Special nonabrasive dirt had to be ordered to backfill the propane tank and the electric lines. We don't often think of nonabrasive dirt; this soft and very finely sifted substance is one of the unknown mysteries to house owners.

Deryl ordered the shoji panels, and as if this were a summons the Japanese ofuro tub arrived. The plumber tested the heating system hydronics with air and found everything good, the Warmboard ready to cover with flooring. Outside there seemed to be as many trenches as in World War I: the grey water line, the power line to the pump, the propane tank line to the house, the satellite cable trench, in addition to the well and septic trenches.

Apparently in early August I said okay to the ceiling lights after a discussion about materials. Jim Petrie had suggested amber-colored mica sheets shaped into cones. The mica sheets he brought looked very handsome, but the cone shape was talk only, I thought, expecting to see sample shades. The next time I saw Jim he was carrying in boxes and boxes and boxes of laboriously fashioned but weirdly unattractive mica light shades. Everyone else liked them but to me they looked like giant moths. The Polygal windows and frames arrived at Gerald's shop, and a few days later the heart pine flooring arrived. Beautiful stuff!

The James Gang kept searching for subcontractors who could put a single rough coat of plain plaster on the walls. Again and again they heard "no." A strange question arose— did I want a doorbell signal in the master bedroom? I did not, especially as there was no doorbell.

In the third week of August 2006 twenty cows waded down the river, climbed ashore at the far end and began gnawing and trampling—cause for yet another Great Cow Chase. Summer fires were burning somewhere and the air was thick and hazed with smoke. We could smell the charring forest but see no flames. Everyone prayed that the Sierra Madre and Medicine Bow ranges would not flare up. Both ranges were mostly dry tinder and standing dead trees. People in nearby Ryan Park, surrounded by thousands of dead red lodgepole, spent sleepless nights.

We abandoned the plans for a scratch coat of plaster—the first rough layer of plaster put over wall lath as a base for the finer finish coats in the days before drywall was invented. The quoted prices for what was once a low-cost undercoat had increased to what one might pay an imported craftsman for hand-painted frescoes. We settled for painted drywall. Gerald set early October for the final concrete floor pour. It was not clear to me if Catfish was working with Mr. A or helping him or neither.

While Gerald worked on sheathing the upstairs ceilings, the electrician discovered some good-looking stainless steel pop-up outlets for the kitchen granite counter. When not in use they folded down almost flush with the countertop presenting just a curved gleam of brushed steel. Everyone liked them, even me. Those were beautiful days, only marred by the knowledge that we had passed the budgeted cost of the house. I began selling stock, maybe a good thing considering what was going to happen in the financial world two years later.

In early September, Gerald cleaned up the house in preparation for the much-postponed insulation team. From this point on everything else that happened would be detail, where, of course, the proof of the pudding lies. The insulation looked like fluffy goose down, but was actually a new form of fiberglass with an R-22 rating and high soundproofing score. It all went smoothly. The sheetrockers arrived and confronted the 247 sheets stacked downstairs. Gerald explained how he wanted it hung. They began in the library, worked quickly and were gone in a week.

The floor, as far as anyone knew, was still a Catfish-and–Mr. A project, but there were indications that Catfish had not actually talked with Mr. A or Mr. A with Catfish. Catfish started tying rebar in place in an eighteen-inch-by-eighteen-inch grid for the floor pour. On October 10 Catfish, Gerald and Mr. A all met and agreed on the rules of the game. And there was more palaver about the shoji panels. Gerald estimated it would take another $200,000 to finish the house. Where was I going to get it? I thought of Jack London who ruined himself financially building and buying a house and ranch.

We all went one evening to make dinner in the ranger cabin in the Medicine Bows which I rented for a few days. It had a broken stove but we had a good time anyway and Dennis told a riveting story of catching an angry badger as a boy and clutching it while it struggled, unable to put it down, unable to do anything. A crusty local man came along, took in the situation at a glance, reached in the back of his truck, pulled out a roll of smooth fence wire, took the badger from Dennis and swiftly wrapped it up in coils like the neck of a Benin princess.

We met with Mr. A concerning the color of the floor. I wanted a deep orange-red that was called Adobe. Everyone was all smiles, for if there was a known factor in this process it was Mr. A's expertise with stained concrete floors. The pour was set for Friday, October 20. Catfish would be on hand. The concrete was confirmed, the pumper truck hired and the site was ready.

Catfish led the concrete and pumper trucks to the house and helped Mr. A lay and muck the floor, hot work that had everyone sweating despite the wind and blowing snow outside. The only good thing about the weather was that it froze the muddy road hard. The plumber watched anxiously in case there was a hydronic leak in the underfloor heating system, but all was well. The next day Mr. A cut the expansion joints which would keep the concrete from cracking. Gerald pointed out some bad areas in the concrete and Mr. A said he would fix them when he came to apply the stain in a few weeks.

A herd of 150 elk moved through Bird Cloud. We heard they had been bunched on the far side of the highway four or five miles distant; then shooting began and they took off to the west, coming straight through Bird Cloud. Gerald called them a good omen.

At the paint store in Laramie we settled on a color for the wall paint. I had used some taupe-colored paint in the Centennial office area and still had some left over. These days paint stores can precisely match your color chips or samples and we got the paint duplicated, a kind of chameleon color that subtly changed hue and intensity according to the time of day, nearby objects, paintings, metamorphosing through shades of mushroom, dry grass, olive, biscuit. It was beautiful and I was entirely consoled for the abandonment of the scratch plaster finish.

The end was in sight and Gerald made what must have been a satisfying list for him writing "Done Done Done" on his checklist. But the Gang had been unable to locate good interior doors at a reasonable price, so they decided they would make them—plank-construction hickory with strap hinges. What is the rarest door in North America? Plank-construction hickory. Somehow they didn't sound very attractive until I saw them—pale, wax-gleaming oversize doors that looked like fine furniture. Like everything else under Gerald's perfectionist hand they were the highest quality work. But there was a new constraint. We had buyers for the Centennial house and they wanted possession by mid-December. A moving day had to be set whether or not Bird Cloud was finished.

Mr. A was scheduled to stain the concrete floor on a Thursday. The day before, Gerald pulled up the tarps to check out the work. He was not pleased with what he saw—a rough surface scarred by the ripples called "chatter." Behind the kitchen range the concrete was too deep and the gas valve had to be moved. Mr. A set to work doing repairs and showed us an acid-stain sample of rich color. Gerald, now very distrustful, watched Mr. A from a distance while the acid stain went on. A few days later Mr. A planned to seal the floor twice and be done.

I drove over early on Friday morning eager to see the beautiful new floor. My God! My God! What a terrible sight. The floor was the color of raw liver and shone greasily as though coated with Vaseline. Mr. A had put on a gloss finish instead of the semigloss. Worst of all, great sweeping arcs of rough concrete and chatter still marred the surface. The floor was lumpy. I did not cry but I felt like it.

Gerald called Mr. A and told him it was a bad floor, but when he called later to set up a meeting Mr. A did not answer his telephone. As it happened there was another floor man—Mr. Floorfix—working on a project in Saratoga at that time and the Gang asked him if he could fix Mr. A's botched job. It was close to Thanksgiving and Mr. Floorfix said he had missed several Thanksgivings and he doubted his wife would let it happen again. But he would ask.

We were all on tenterhooks. After an anxious day Deryl got the message that Mr. Floorfix's family agreed he could squeeze the job into his nightmare schedule. His price was severe—$40,000 (unbudgeted) compared to Mr. A's $11,000 (budgeted)—but we were over a barrel. Mr. Floorfix said the lumpy surface had to be ground down, densified and restained, twice the work that Mr. A did, and the grinding would take time. He had "green" colors and had made up some samples for me to see. Burnt Sienna looked the closest to Mr. A's attractive Adobe acid stain. But Mr. Floorfix's sample colors on chunks of concrete from our floor (Deryl dug up waste pieces from the hole in which he had buried them) were pale and not attractive, apparently because there was more limestone in our concrete which affected the color. I said I had really liked Mr.

A's Adobe color and Mr. Floorfix said no problem, he would use acid stain. As he was leaving he mentioned that the grinding process would reveal the aggregate stone chips in the concrete mix below. That meant the floor would have a speckled semi-terrazzo appearance, a look I have never liked. Mr. Floorfix was able to start a day earlier than we hoped, but the schedule for installing the kitchen cabinets and the countertops was now in shambles.

The stain Mr. A had put on the floor had barely penetrated, so there was less grinding needed which didn't translate into any cost reduction. The Gang roasted a turkey with fixin's for Mr. Floorfix and his crew in appreciation of their effort on a national holiday. Still unable to reach Mr. A, Gerald sent a certified letter mentioning the word "lawyer," and Mr. A responded, saying the floor finish was the best he could do except maybe waxing it. Gerald said the finish was not the big problem—except that the sealer was glossy instead of matte—that wax wasn't needed. The problem was the rotary polisher marks and the dirt, rocks, sand and Sheetrock fragments rolled into the top finish.

Meanwhile Mr. Floorfix was grinding away. Mr. A made a surprise visit to see what the complaints were all about, but at this point Mr. Floorfix had ground the evidence off. Mr. A was furious.

Alas, Mr. Floorfix was no champion. He told Gerald he didn't have the tools to fix the corners so the Gang had to get out their air chisels and spend hours doing it for him. The first coat of stain went on and it looked good. Gerald, however, no longer had any faith in concrete floor people and was watching Mr. Floorfix suspiciously. The second coat of stain went on. The next step was to neutralize the acid and spray on the densifier.

Was there no end to this disaster? Mr. Floorfix's acid stain came out a repulsive yellow-orange color. We decided that a half-strength "mahogany" dye would fix the problem. It had to fix it as we were out of time and the money was gone. Mr. Floorfix and his team worked all night dyeing the floor and putting on densifier. The final result was a dusty, dull brownish red speckled floor. Mr. Floorfix warned that no sealer could go on for months and that the floor had to be wet-mopped frequently to take up the unwanted acid stain that would work to the surface. He wasn't kidding. For the next year I swabbed the huge floor several times a week, the rough concrete dust wearing out shoes and socks, destroying the mop, and still the floor threw off red dust. Eventually the dust was minimal and we called Mr. Floorfix to ask about putting on a sealer but he said the floor should not be sealed at all. This made no sense as the floor was as ugly as dried mud. By contrast, upstairs the heart pine floors went in, stained and oiled four times. They were a joy, though Gerald got a headache from the fumes which he (a teetotaler) likened to a hangover.

We were down to counting days before the move from Centennial and Bird Cloud fairly steamed in the chilly December air from the violent activity inside. The house became a mad blur of rushing people, Dennis building cabinets, Lindsay hammering book stacks together and cleaning the walls that were dusty from Mr. Floorfix's grinding extravaganza, Doug installing the glowing kitchen cabinets and pantry shelves, the plumber and the electrician climbing and crawling, the metal baseboard going on, Gerald weather-stripping the garage doors, the refrigerator jostled into place, doorjambs and trim going on, the tile man cleaning up grout and silicone. It was only a little more than a week until Roughrider Movers (aptly named) would come with the furniture from Centennial. And before the furniture, hundreds of boxes of books had to be moved. My job.

In Centennial day after day I packed books and Uphill Bob loaded them into Gerald's multipurpose snowmobile trailer. The James Gang somehow found time to drive it over to Bird Cloud and Lindsay and I and a husky high school kid unloaded the endless cartons. The fun of shelving began, a job not finished three years later.

Roughrider Movers used several trucks crammed to bursting with *stuff*—lawn mowers, suitcases, dressers, computers, hangers, pictures, cartons of china, kitchen pots and pans, beds, mattresses, musical instruments, sports equipment, file cabinets, desks and tables, chairs and more chairs, garden hoses, the contents of a full attic including masses of goods belonging to my children. I decided to move the dozens of framed paintings and photographs myself rather than have the Roughriders sling them around. These movers did a very bad thing that I did not discover until months later. In the Centennial attic I had forty-odd boxes of manuscripts and drafts. The boxes were cataloged, labeled and taped shut. One of the mover-helpers, without asking, decided to open and repack the boxes more economically to save space. If he were to appear before me now I would kill him.

It was a builder's nightmare, the owner moving in before the house was finished, but I had no choice. The James Gang made no complaint and kept on working. In fact they were months, even years away from being finished. We learned to live with each other.

My sons Jon, Gillis and Morgan arrived and Jon's wife Gail for a truly weird Christmas celebration. Nothing was unpacked and moving around was a matter of sucking in your stomach and sidling through the narrow aisles between boxes.

It was like a scavenger hunt as the Roughriders had mislabeled almost every box. A carton that was marked "bed linen" might hold two sheets, a coffee grinder, fragile lamps, vases, a box of matches and seven shoes. Doing anything in the kitchen was difficult as there were still no counters, just sagging pieces of scrap plywood to get us through.

It was cold. And it began to snow. Hard. The battle to get in and out over the snow-clogged, drift-packed county road began. I was shocked and frightened to learn that the road was not maintained in winter, contrary to the real estate agent's assurances three years earlier.

Despite the welter of unpacked boxes, blowing snow and cold, when I came downstairs in the morning the great cliff filled the windows, radiant and bulging forward. All difficulties were forgotten as the rising sun drenched it in luminous yellow. Rockwell Kent in *N by E* remarked, "We *live* for those fantastic and unreal moments of beauty which our thoughts may build upon the passing panorama of experience."[1]

1. Rockwell Kent, *N by E* (New York: Brewer and Warren, 1930), 16.

CHAPTER 7

Details, Details, Details

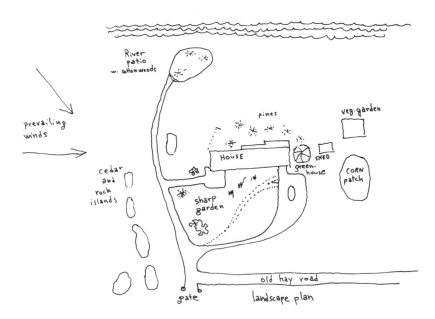

2006–2007

It was Christmas and Jon and Gail, Gillis, Morgan and I were in
the house, unable to find roasting pans or silverware, everyone
jammed into odd corners, vehicles getting stuck in the snow,
some sliding into deep ditches, some unable to move at all, wind
howling. I lost it when someone stuck the old Land Cruiser
half in the deepest ditch so that it teetered horribly on the verge

117

of tipping upside down and maiming my nearest and dearest. Hack, of Hack's Tackle, came with his plow and got stuck himself. The James Gang came to rescue Hack and got enough snow out of the way so that Gillis could escape the heavy drifts. Gillis fled south and we all wished we could follow him.

The James Gang, in between hours of working on the house, plowed the white stuff. More snow fell. Again and again I heard the voice of The Nature Conservancy's real estate agent answering my early question "Is the county road maintained in winter?" with a clear, confident "yes." I think he honestly believed they plowed this back road, but I wish he had checked, because for me it was a serious problem. I now had a new house that had taken all my money and that was inaccessible to wheeled vehicles in snowy winters. By the time spring came I understood very well that spending winters at Bird Cloud would be impossible. Everything changed as I realized I would be semihomeless from October through March. Later it dawned on me that I would still have to heat the empty house.

But the Japanese soak tub was in place, clean and ready to use, the massive heater in the adjacent closet turned on. That evening I filled the tub with hot water. I had been looking forward to this for two years. The long soak was wonderful, but an hour later, I discovered a terrible flood in the library. Water had cascaded all over the file cabinets and floor and swelled the wall paint into an enormous blister. A hysterical call brought the James Gang out. They discovered that the outflow drain had frozen up. Fortunately very little water got inside the file cabinets and four people violently mopping and swabbing got the water cleaned up with no bad damage. But Gerald decided to install a different drain system.

On the last day of January, Dave went in for surgery on his ankle. While he was being prepped, he complained of a stomachache. Nothing was simple. The stomachache turned out to be appendicitis. The docs removed the offending organ and the ankle fusing was scheduled for the future when he was hale and hearty again. While all this was happening my wonderful assistant, Lindsay Ricketts, went to Texas to visit her family and I planned to go to Santa Fe to visit Gillis and escape the snow for a week.

In the days before I left, the wind was like a carpenter's plane shaving long strips of snow-filled air off the side of the house and the pale face of the cliff. Those strips curled and tangled in turbulence of extraordinary velocity. More and more snow came and the James Gang couldn't make it out to the house. They worked on doors in Gerald's shop. As soon as the weather cleared they roared in on snowmobiles. When I got back from New Mexico the Wyoming weather had improved. Briefly. On and on went the finish work on the hundreds of small details. The copper ceilings went up in the family room, the entryway and fishing room, the shiny metal softened with a patina that suggested subtle aging. The plank walls were a mellow, warm color like Darjeeling tea, stained with a vinegar and steel wool pad recipe from Doug Ricketts. And the snow and wind kept coming. Relentlessly.

We waited for the reverse osmosis water purification system. By error the whole outfit went to Kansas where it was passed along to another freight company that suffered a break-in and wouldn't have another guard until the next day. Don't call us, we'll call you. But finally all of it arrived in early March which is not springtime in Wyoming but the snowiest month. Gerald kept smashing a path through the drifts on the county road and managed to get in and out most days, taking a risk lover's joy in the nauseating slides toward the ditch, the scrape of ice and packed snow on his truck's undercarriage. Deryl ran the skid steer up and down the lane constantly, working the blower overtime. From a mile away you could see a great plume of snow arcing into the grey air.

At this point I was close to broke and asked, How much longer? How much more money? Gerald promised figures and dates soon and kept putting up the copper ceiling in the family room. We did not know it then but he had scratched the names of all our family on the panels. They were impossible to see. Everything had been far more expensive than the budget.

I understood the need to get the work finished, but the late hours and lack of privacy were driving me mad. I asked the plumber and electrician to leave one night and everyone's nose was out of joint. They were doing me a favor by working long, hard hours, and I, instead of being appreciative, complained. Trying to write, trying to think, even trying to live in the midst of incessant construction made me terminally irritable. God, would it ever be done? How much better it would have been if I had been able to stay in the old house until the end of the work on this one. This is why house owners take long ocean voyages until construction is quite finished.

On a March weekend when the James Gang had a snowmobile holiday there was an accident and Lindsay broke her arm, a bad break that would refuse to heal properly. Late in the month, by some miracle of climate change, the paved roads to and from the outside world were clear and Jim Petrie came up. I complained that the mechanical room made a lot of noise that reverberated both downstairs and upstairs. The Sub-Zero refrigerator was noisy as well. The Sierra Pacific window screens did not fit and the electrician said the only thing to do was make new ones. So be it, dammit.

I had a talk with the James Gang about the cost overruns and Gerald opined that the architects should pay the difference as problems in the design had needed remedial work to make the house functional. Maybe all architects design buildings that are primarily about appearance. Didn't some of Frank Lloyd Wright's houses have leaky roofs? And as much as with the architect, the problems lay with the suppliers who sent wrong or ill-fitting parts. I think, too, that Gerald, who had rarely worked with architects, was under the impression that all problems would be solved in advance in the design on paper. Then, when a problem did arise and the James Gang saw a way to fix it, Harry's attitude toward proposed modifications was not always cooperative. Both sides—adversarial when the paper plans did not match wood or metal reality—could have been more open and listened to each other, but I'm the last one who should complain that others were not cooperative enough. Gerald mentioned that he hoped the time would come when he could sit down with Harry and explain some construction procedures that couldn't work as drawn on the plans. And Harry had a little list of items that he thought Gerald should have known.

The Augustan architect Marcus Vitruvius Pollio is regarded today more as a figurehead father of architecture than someone whose views on houses belong in the pages of *Dwell* or *Wallpaper,* but there is something terribly obvious about his three general precepts in *De Architectura* that have held true over two thousand years: that an architect-designed building must have integrity of structure, a responsibility to function, and the added delight of beauty. Included in those precepts might be enhanced landscaping, and, as we discover today, in the first years of the third millennium, the necessity of making energy-efficient, water-thrifty houses overrides everything else. There is no choice. Buildings must operate within stricter "green" bounds.

Many architects also seem more concerned with self-expression as artists, or the chance to pursue an intellectual exercise rather than cater to a client's presumed desires. So there is the question of warring egos, and even if the anti-pathetical positions are never voiced, they lurk dangerously beneath the surface. Architects think differently than clients might expect. For example, Thom Mayne, one of the founders of the California architects' group, Morphosis, remarked on "real architecture":

> The business of architecture serves clients. You go out there and you find out what clients need today—what are they interested in today? Real architecture is the antithesis of that. Your interests are more private and personal over an extended period of time and require an independence which is akin to leadership. It is up to you to define the issues. I am not interested in fashion or even in the look of the work. I am interested in starting ideas that take you someplace, and in the process, the methodological process. You have to build to get feedback. Some people start with the visual or physiognomic characteristics. They work toward manifesting that vision. I don't work that way. I work with concepts that build to something. I don't know where I am going. . . . Materials are chosen very late. It has to do with lines and directions and forces that have nothing to do with appearance. It is not easy to deal with clients because most of them are not at all interested in the investigation.[1]

I noted the emphasis on "today," implying that the clients are flighty creatures who may well have different interests tomor-

---

1. Philip Jodidio, *New Forms: Architecture in the 1990s* (New York: Taschen, 2001), 28.

row. Nor do clients, including this one, always know what they really want in the structure. I had been sure I wanted a writing area without eye-level windows so I would not be distracted by bird-watching or the view. I got that room and now often carry my work to the dining room with the large windows where I can look outside. A window in the work area would have been better. And I have always liked rooms with high ceilings, but there is an atmosphere of chill remoteness that comes with such space.

A favorite book of mine is Bernard Rudofsky's 1964 *Architecture Without Architects,* photographs of some of the world's most vernacular dwellings, including the rodentlike holes of an old burial ground in Siwa, Egypt, which people have taken over as housing, hollow baobab trees, the stone-cone *trulli* of Apulia, the clawed-out rock houses of Les Baux-en-Provence, and, in Anatolia, the adaptation of volcanic formations to dwellings. They seem springboards of ideas rather than models outside of fortuitous local geology, but from what I've learned of American Indian pit houses, many such vernacular dwellings were efficient and sensible for their locations.

Something that seems to irritate all architects is the basic fact that buildings (except for nomads' tents) are fixed. Many avant-garde structures have complex angles and thrusts that indicate motion such as a bird frozen in flight or the "exploded isometric projection" of Zaha Hadid's Vitra Fire Station, or Eric Owen Moss's "The Box" with its violent twists and "bronco attic," or Peter Eisenman's unbuilt Möbius strip double-tower house. Those few buildings of stunning visual impact that were actually constructed suited the period of computer-aided design and surplus wealth that allowed experimentation. Although I find innovative architecture extremely interesting, I did not have the money to play that game. Bird Cloud's site had its own powerful forces—the cliff that dominated the immediate and surrounding region, and, at its foot, the islanded North Platte River, and, above all, the wind. Were it not for the wind, the snow would not be an insoluble problem.

The decision to build near the entrance at the lower southwest part of the property answered the expectation of the house serving as a year-round dwelling. It was the most economical site and had the most dramatic view of the cliff. The southeast area, in the trees, was more beautiful and secluded, but would have added another mile to the site entrance and called for a bridge over an old river channel that became impassably wet in springtime. Hindsight is cheap, but if I had known the unexpected and undisclosed problems of the chosen site I would not have bought the property.

At the end of March, after a period of clear skies, all the roads were again closed by blowing, hard-packed snow, reinforcing the winter limitations of the site. On April Fool's Day the mechanical room still wasn't finished and the pumps in it made an amount of noise that was especially obnoxious in the guest room upstairs. Gerald thought it was the solar pumps that made the noise, but later we decided it was the lack of sound-deadening rubber cushions between the various pumps and the walls and concrete slab. Harry said (but had neglected to put this in the plans, assuming the contractor would know it) that separating the machine room section of the slab from the main house would have greatly reduced the noise, for sound travels through concrete rather well. Some noise persisted. When Harry visited the house a few years later he remarked that the culprit was the pipes, especially the pipes from the main pump on the floor, and that by draining and cutting them and inserting short rubber interrupter sections the noise would be dampened. He remarked that the plumber and/or builder should have known this and have done it automatically. But this is Wyoming and such arcane knowledge hadn't yet reached the mountains.

Work on the windows continued through the spring of 2007, punctuated by visits to various doctors for Lindsay (broken arm), Deryl (spine), osteo surgeon for Dave, the chiropractor for Gerald, the dentist for me. The battle of the trespass cows continued on the far side of the river and the island. To chase cows off the far shore we paddled across the river, leapt out and ran cursing through the cottonwoods. A bridge across the North Platte would have been a huge help and we made idle talk about the possibility of buying the beautiful old Pick Bridge downriver, still in place though superseded by a standard concrete bridge. Dave remarked that it had been for sale some time ago and perhaps still was. A monster helicopter could lift and carry it a mile to Bird Cloud. Then we found out the bridge was not for sale but had been designated a National Register property—a good thing as it is a fine example of a nineteenth-century iron truss design and more handsome than any concrete wannabe.

There were more doctor trips and more cow chasing. I talked with the James Gang about finding an unemployed cowboy to chase the critters away, but that was a pipe dream, not a practical solution. Unfortunately more fencing was needed, especially around the island. I'd rather have had a cow chaser than more fence, but fence doesn't take any days off and it is never late. Damn living in an open range state where cows can wander where they want. Ranchers have dominated the laws and affairs of this state since the Territorial days. Fencing cows *in* will not become Wyoming law until there is a major shift in mind-set, until more people do not want cows trampling around their houses. That may underlie the state's antipathy toward newcomers, for they are the unreasonable souls who would like to flout open range tradition. But the good news was that the helpful cowboy from the neighboring TA Ranch said the cows would move up to summer pasture on Elk Mountain in a few days.

In late April 2007 the Gang cleared construction materials out of the garage and for the first time I could park vehicles in it. In between the bustle of doors, cabinets, toe kicks and finish details Gerald helped me hang pictures to get them out of the way. It warmed up one weekend and friends came for supper and we grilled steaks. Springtime in the Rockies.

In May the work continued. One of the strange design problems was the placement in the floor of several electrical outlets downstairs. In the living-dining room area they were directly in the traffic corridor and someone was always tripping on them. They were unattractive and useless, as plugging anything in meant the traffic hazard of trailing cords. Sanding, varnishing, prepping, priming, caulking, hanging, installing, patching, mudding, trimming, drilling, assembling, capping went on and on and I fled to Ireland.

By the time I got back the giant snowplows had opened the Medicine Bow Pass between Centennial and the Saratoga Road, and the Gang had made me a vegetable garden with mole-proof underlay, a watering system, topsoil and some rotted manure from retired Dr. L's manure heap on the east side of the valley. I was thrilled. For the past decade I had been barred from having a garden by the rules of the Centennial homeowners' association. I grew up in a gardening family and I have almost always had a vegetable garden myself. I deplore the stale produce and food conglomerate cans of mush sold in too many western grocery stores. It was a good day when Whole Foods opened a store in Fort Collins and I shopped there once a month despite the long, long drive and high prices. Now I studied the seed catalogs planning to grow everything from eggplants to *cavalo nero,* a dark and bitter Italian kale. In fact I became enamored of an Italian seed company and bought too many packets of seeds that needed a Mediterranean climate. We'd see what they could do in a challenging place, though the San Marzano tomatoes had to go in the greenhouse. I was not so lucky with this company the next year for a packet proclaiming the contents were seeds of small white eggplants turned out to be cantaloupes. Curses!

One May day the James Gang and I and the archaeologist Dudley Gardner, who had dropped in, all took an afternoon to go down to the immigrant crossing where '49ers and Overland Trail parties crossed the North Platte. To get there we went through the vast Overland Ranch owned by Anschutz, reportedly the site for the world's largest wind turbine farm. There are many very large ranches in this part of Wyoming owned by corporate executives and heirs, including such household names as Ciba-Geigy, Anschutz, Wal-Mart, Campbell's Foods. On the way we saw swathes of Indian paintbrush, Wyoming's state flower, most a deep orange-red color, some a lighter red or orange and a few yellow. Deryl remarked that when he and his brothers were kids they could still see bits and pieces of broken wagons and discarded items along the road which was, in fact, an important section of the Overland Trail. At the crossing in the period from 1840 to 1860 there was a rope-operated ferry that hauled wagon parties across the river.

There was a small cemetery on the bluff above the crossing, fenced to provide some protection from the ever-present vandals. Something there is in the human character that burns to destroy the past or carry it home. A few hundred yards from the trail was a steep and narrow declivity like something out of a Tony Hillerman story. We inched our way down and walked along the overgrown trail below the bluff, then returned along the riverbank. Archaeologist Dudley, who was with us, looked closely at the bank where the river had eaten away the soil and found a handsome stone knife. Later, in the Red Desert, we found stone tools and an exquisite Eden projectile point of deep red stone, a rarity, the continent's most beautful prehistoric point. I found several fossilized bones. The University of Wyoming had no paleontologist, so I took them to the New Mexico Museum of Natural History; the largest piece was the toe bone of an Eocene mammal, impossible to identify without a tooth.

On a Saturday in early June, when the wind was unaccountably calm, we drove up to the top of the Bird Cloud cliff. There were plenty of mosquitoes. Prairie dogs sat straight up, one foot in the burrow, watching us warily. The cushion plants along the edge of the cliff and down a sloping section of its face bloomed thousands of puffy mounds of tiny flowers, white, blue, yellow, deep pink. I especially liked the *Eriogonums,* wild buckwheat. Indian paintbrush was everywhere in profuse four color blossom, goldflower and yellow stonecrop, miner's candles and phlox, white forget-me-nots and intense purple-blue lupines. On the way back down to the house in late afternoon we passed the great horned owl's favorite log, the owl dozing until it would be time to get up and terrorize the night.

We sat by the river slapping mosquitoes that ignored our smudge fire smoke and cheered on the swallow ballet pursuing the insects over the river corridor. Knots of bird exploded, coalesced, twisted in ribbons, doubled and slid sideways, mounted in loose circles, became winged bobbins hurtling through a random warp of mosquitoes. Their numbers increased until, in the orange afterglow of sunset, thousands and thousands were gliding past the cliff's vertical canyons and crevasses.

The next day Uphill Bob from Centennial came over and we put up the bluebird houses he had made, rather fancy, one with an inset glass eye that reminded me of the nineteenth-century whaling ships that had heavy glass prisms set flush in the decks (flat side up) to admit light to the crews' quarters below. At dusk I went up again to the top of the cliff. The sky was filling with clouds trailing long fingers like rake tines. A golden eagle flew past at eye level, a limp prairie dog in its talons.

Lindsay continued to work on cataloging and shelving the books, two systems that did not match up very well. Now, years later, I wish we had cataloged the books differently. The database is awkward to use. Categories blur and overlap, and it is difficult to find the book I want unless I remember the author's name or the exact title. I often do not, looking instead for a book I remember as having a pale blue cracked spine and standing near a volume on raptors. One of my dreams, not likely to be realized, is to have the library recataloged by a librarian who will ignore my wrongheaded ideas about shelving categories.

The summer quickly heated up and, as usual, no one could remember the bitter winter storms. In mid-June, when the river was high and galloping along, we floated it with my wildlife habitat friend Ron Lockwood and the ornithologist Andrea Orabona who was doing an eagle count. Ron's truck's U-joint had seized up on the way in and while we looked for eagles Dave and Deryl got it repaired.

Hot, hot, hot, edging into the nineties, days for cold watermelon down by the river. And when night fell the heat trapped inside the house was terrific. The south-facing Polygal windows invited the burning rays in and the walls held the heat. It didn't seem to cool off at night until Harry said to open the downstairs windows on the north side and the upstairs south windows every evening. This started a column of deliciously cool air moving through the house. The Polygal windows had another annoying feature: the frames expanded in the morning and contracted at night with sudden loud pops and snaps as though someone were trying to break in with a pry bar. Harry said the cure was to loosen the frames which were likely too tight. So once again Gerald climbed up and loosened the frame screws a little. The violent snapping subsided to soft coughs but never completely disappeared. On hot sunny days the Polygal frames still make a slight shifting sound as if they were trying to stretch.

Day after day siding went on, the constant *pow! pow!* of the nail gun more familiar than the wind. Gerald kept on working through the heat and four days after the July Fourth parades and fireworks the siding was finished. It was time for the chinkers to come and fill in the interstices between the planks. And Lindsay, after four months of pain, finally had surgery on her broken arm which had not healed.

The electrician discovered that Mr. Solar had committed a code violation in the mechanical room, and repaired it. When Gerald called Mr. Solar he tried to brush it off with a comment to the effect, So what, it's Wyoming, isn't it? The belief many outsiders have is that anything goes in a place with a rough-and-tumble reputation, but that only applies to the cow business. Many Wyoming entities and businesses are punctilious about rules. A few weeks later the electrician asked the state inspector to check the solar installation work and his repair. Everything passed.

Chink, chink, chink, chinking, chink some more, chink on, chink from ten until six, chink in the moonlight, chink, order more chink material, clean the chink gun, chink, chink, chink. Ye gods, chink on, ever on. If the guys were sick of chinking

I was desperate for them to *get done* even though there was no noise in the work. It seemed eternities had passed since Catfish had poured the slab. The chinking seemed the longest and most tedious part of the entire construction menu, but in late July it was truly finished. Almost.

Gerald, in one of his flourishes, had put up a yardarm extending out from under the eaves at the east end of the house—a sheltered vantage point for an owl. The owls liked the house but they spurned the yardarm in preference to the roof ridge above my bedroom. The resident great horned owls disappeared the next year and a pair of barn owls moved onto the island to make the nights hideous with their croaking calls. One twilight evening, watching the resident jackrabbit gobbling clover, I noticed one of the owls teetering on the top strand of a wire fence around the front "sharp" garden (so called because it had a dozen yuccas in it). Then the owl launched itself at the rabbit, twisting down on it, and from the roof ridge came the owl's mate from a different direction. But the rabbit did some pretzel-like acrobatics and escaped the double sets of talons. "It's harder than it looks," I said to the owls who flew away. The rabbit disappeared into the shadows and the next evening returned to the clover patch. Just another day at the office.

After the chinking marathon it was finally time to put the rusted metal siding on the entryways. A sheet of old barn metal lying on the ground does not look like the stuff of dreams, but in combination with the plank siding and neatly enclosing the entryways it looked entirely right. We were all so pleased with the success of the entryways that we went back to the top of the cliff, archaeological clues marking a possible ancient bison jump.

The Gang could not stop. The house was essentially finished but the "yard" outside was remarkably similar to a gravel pit. When the wind blew, fine dust was hurled against the windows and when it blew hard, small gravel rattled the house. There was no place one could sit outside in comfort, so we planned a deck on the north of the house using the leftover planks, dreaming of cool shadows and quiet evenings. Deryl and I had some discussions about turning the gravel pit area into a landscaped garden. Because of the gravelly, alkaline soil it seemed a good idea to plant clover which would ameliorate the alkalinity and build up the soil. Deryl thought it a good idea to sow ryegrass around the house in the fall and clover the next spring. The idea seemed sensible. We couldn't guess what a monster we were going to create, for the clover went berserk, grew like wildfire in a strong wind and needed cutting every week, a hard job that involved moving the wire fence circles around all the trees. Furthermore, the clover attracted a herd of deer who also ate the expensive shrubs Deryl had planted.

The deck went together very quickly and by the end of the next day the Gang sanded the planks and made them ready for the vinegar-and-steel-wool stain. Then we could sit outside with a glass of wine.

In late August the stairway handrail went up. The stairs were of the same beautiful distressed heartwood pine as the upstairs floors and fastened down with fancy bronze button nails. One of the most attractive features of the house was only visible from the top of the stairs. In a high, angled alcove above the front entry there was a confluence of intersecting lines, materials and angles. A section of the corrugated rusted metal polished to a soft gleam comes forward at a rakish angle. Behind it, at another angle, runs a strip of blue Polygal window in diminishing perspective that makes me think of Utrillo's streets. Far at the back of the shadowy recess hangs one of the artist Jeff

Fields's headless torsos, a life-size female figure in the flowing garments of another century. I'd had this piece for several years but had never realized until it was placed at Bird Cloud, that it glowed with a faint blue iridescent light echoing the Polygal windows. It worked so well it seemed to have been made for the space. This one small area, with its interesting slices and bands of light, its varied textures, its harmonious strangeness, gives the journey down the stairs a little zing of pleasure.

My old fishing pal, Tom, came to visit in August. We went to the top of Kennaday Peak where Tom found good cell phone reception, visited the James Gang's lodge site in Battle Pass. Years before, in Newfoundland, Tom had built a table for me from old boards pulled from the ancient and collapsing fish house on the shore. It was one of the few things I salvaged from the Newfoundland house, and it had been waiting in storage for two years. Now Tom put the legs back on and the old spruce boards, tempered by time, salt and sea, began a new life as an outside sorting table for archaeological and geological finds. The same day the table came back to life we discovered cows on the east end of the property, cows that had waded down the river. We drove them back into the water, and I, still thinking about Newfoundland, wished for lashing, salty waves. (In truth there were cows who swam in the ocean in Newfoundland near the island where the abandoned town of Fortune rotted away.) The week closed with a merry dinner with Tom, the James Gang and Mr. B, a friend from Centennial. I got out the glass bota that a friend had given me years before and filled it with Mr. B's red wine. It was rather fun, passing it around, and everyone—even Gerald, unable to resist a contest, who abandoned his Mountain Dew habit for the evening—went home with a stained shirt.

At the end of August the James Gang went off to Mount

Antero in Colorado's Sawatch Range, their annual geological expedition and vacation, something they've done for years. They have often described the trip up the mountain over a narrow hairpin road with steep drop-offs, no place to turn around, snow, mud and ice and violent lightning. It is accessible only for a few weeks in summer before the wind and snow close the perilous track.

For almost a year several times a week I mopped the ugly and very large floor. We called Mr. Floorfix frequently to ask when we could put sealer on the floor. "Not yet! Not yet!" he kept saying although we told him the mop water was no longer picking up thrown-off stain, and the floor was everlastingly dull and dusty. It was really ugly and ruined the house. I began to think we would have to do everything over again, move all fifty-six bookcases, each weighing hundreds of pounds, and put something—what?—on top of the speckled, dusty mess. I started to think about tiles.

In September, Pearl, the James Gang's mother, died. Somehow, in the midst of all the building and work, they had cared and cooked for her and now she was gone. The funeral service was packed and the little memorial leaflet, instead of the usual poem about heading into the sunset, featured Pearl's secret recipe for her famous fried chicken.

Although the house was finished, the geodesic dome I used as a greenhouse, which the Gang had disassembled and moved from Centennial, lay in pieces under a large tarp. Now came the mind-twisting puzzle of putting it back together. Wyoming is a tough place to grow vegetables as summer hailstorms and frosts and strong winds make growing anything except herbs, carrots and beets a silly dream. But gardening is an important part of life for me. The Growing Dome greenhouse, the invention of two Scots, Udgar and Pujga Parsons in Pagosa

Springs, Colorado, was the answer. A Buckminster Fuller–inspired low-cost geodesic dome designed for gardening in the Rocky Mountains, it is one of the best objects I ever acquired. For fourteen years I have grown tomatoes, lettuces, cucumbers, eggplant and other tender crops in one of these excellent structures. In the Centennial location the prevailing westerly wind constantly strained the self-regulating ventilation opener mechanisms and we replaced several. But at Bird Cloud the structure was in a more sheltered setting and there were no problems with the openers. We regularly have ripe tomatoes by mid-July. In open gardens it is a race with the season to have even faintly pink tomatoes by September. My only complaint about the dome is that I should have bought a larger size.

We still had storage problems, so in October, while the good weather held, the Gang poured the foundation for a shed to hold garden tools, vehicle tires, canoe, kayak, plant pots, camping equipment, tools, wire fence and a hundred other items that would not fit into either the garage or the fishing room. The building went up quickly and Gerald insulated it in case I ever wanted to turn it into a guesthouse. *Not!*

The driveway to the house went in using the same lousy road base material the county used for its back ways, a kind of fine gravel and sand with no clay to bind it together. It never firmed up and tires gradually worked the material to the sides of the road. It was poor stuff compared to New England dirt roads that pack down smooth and hard because there is clay content. But there was nothing else and we put it on the half-mile lane that leads to the house from the county road, hoping it would improve the alkali mud and river rock of the original lane. The next year we brought in several loads of crushed stone which, judiciously placed, made a firmer surface.

We tried a rented floor-cleaning machine on the damn dusty

red floor. Gerald's understatement was that "it didn't work too good," and he took off elk hunting. It snowed and after the snow melted Deryl scratched up a few acres on the east end where rampant cheatgrass had grown until Mr. Bromley, the weed control wizard from Encampment, had sprayed it earlier in the year. This was an area we hoped to put back into native grasses. Deryl sowed inland salt grass seed at the suggestion of a Game and Fish adviser and we hoped for a wet spring. Suddenly autumn was finished and here came cold, blowing snow, plenty of winter weather. We had a final dinner at the Wolf Hotel for Lindsay Ricketts to see her off to Denver and a new career. Dave and Deryl took off to Florida. And I headed for Santa Fe.

In Santa Fe that winter I found an answer to Bird Cloud's ugly floor. I had the habit of walking around the town in the mornings, and on one of those walks I passed a stone yard that specialized in floor tiles. It was closed but I went again a week later during business hours. There were so many tiles in so many rich colors that I was bewildered until I saw several very large (twenty-four-inch-square) slate tiles the color of the Atlantic ocean in deep water, a liquid blue-green. I knew at once that these would suit Bird Cloud and make the horrible floor beautiful. They could also cover the unwanted floor outlets. After several phone consultations with the James Gang— Could it be done? Could the full bookcases be moved without removing the books? What was the floor area?—I placed the order. Indeed, overordered at Gerald's request to allow for breakage. Because the tiles had to come from Brazil there would be a wait of many months.

That summer when the heavy crates arrived we all crowded around as Gerald pried the lid off the first box. There was a moment of horror when he took out the first tiles. They were rough and unfinished. I had ordered brushed tiles, neither milled completely flat, nor rough, but smooth and with an interesting slight texture visible to the eye but not the touch. I went inside, sure that the entire order was wrong, another chapter in the dreadful floor saga. But Deryl came in and said it had been only the first two tiles that were rough. The others were brushed smooth. They were beautiful. In rapture we rushed around putting random tiles down to see how they went with the walls, with the metal baseboard, in the kitchen, the entryway. Everywhere they looked wonderful. Success at last.

I had to go to Germany and while I was gone the James Gang and the tile setter handled the enormous job of moving all the furniture and the full bookcases, of closing off and filling in the unwanted floor outlets, of measuring, cutting and laying the tile. The floor was almost the floor of my dreams, clean, smooth, elegant and a ravishing color. I swore always to have tile floors wherever I lived. The bookcases were perfectly in place. How had they done all this in two weeks? I will never know.

CHAPTER 8

Bird Cloud's Checkered Past

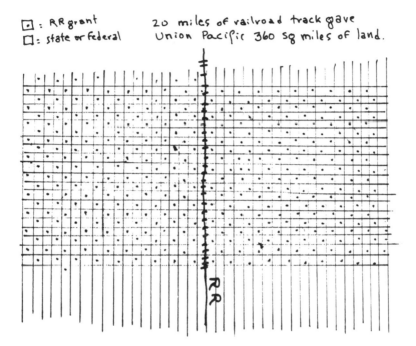

The American government has bruised the people's trust from time to time. One of the most blatant examples was the great nineteenth-century giveaway of huge chunks of public land to a handful of railroad barons in the name of patriotic progress and "opening up the country." Some of those vigorous entrepreneurs dreamed of Far East markets served by a cross-continent rail line.

Among the most rapacious grabbers were English and Scots landed gentry, well-traveled, sophisticated, with keen eyes for profitable situations. North America was a treasure house— timber, minerals, furs, grazing land, big-game trophies—and they knew it. Despite the United States' autonomy, an older sense of a right to exploitation still colored upper-class sensibilities in the British Isles. Today we point accusatory fingers at the most outrageous mining and railroad moguls of the period, but the pervasive ethos of social Darwinism and imperialism, the presumed right of the elite to skim the cream from any country's natural resources, was accepted. Those who took what they wanted were generally admired and envied.

In America the intense desire to accumulate wealth and power was democratized; the wealthy, the highborn, the titled, the poor immigrant boy, the disappointed New England businessman, the dispossessed farmer, the unemployed young man all believed they had a right to the pots of gold at the end of the American rainbow. Dozens of popular books of the period featured poor, barefoot farm boys who became rich through hard work, clever ideas, recognition of opportunities and the wheel-greasing kindness of wealthy men (with blond, blue-eyed daughters). The virtue of "hard work" was often invoked to sugarcoat aggressive, unscrupulous dealings with more naïve people.

The forceful entrepreneurial spirit burned strongly in Canada and the American west. Wyoming remains to this day a kind of juicy natural resources fruit that corporate and business interests feel entitled to squeeze dry. The history of section 21—Bird Cloud—touches both ends of the spectrum. When Wyoming was still a territory a titled Scotsman who had everything owned the Sand Creek Cattle and Land Company ranch abutting what is now Bird Cloud. And before that section 21 was part of a holding bought by a trio of Irish brothers from Vermont who started out with nothing and became powerful and wealthy, the Horatio Alger story come true.

The transcontinental railroad had been talked up as inevitable since the 1830s. Abraham Lincoln put the talk into action, granting subsidies and huge pieces of territory to corporations. Chief among the broadcloth-suited railroad finaglers of the Union Pacific and Central Pacific were Thomas Durant, Jay Cooke, Grenville Dodge, Oliver Ames, Collis Huntington, their relatives, friends and political connections, abetted by a carload of criminal-minded congressmen. Stock manipulations, bribery, "creative" bookkeeping, countless government loans and subsidies and, above all, very large land grants made the great fortunes of a select few.

In 1862 the Union Pacific Rail Road received, along with a right-of-way, more than a thousand miles long through the public domain, a grant of half the lands in a strip ten miles wide on each side of the tracks they promised to lay down. The railroad could do what it wished with these chunks of prairie, forest and mountain. The road extended from Omaha to Promontory Point in Utah where the tracks eventually met up with those of Huntington's Central Pacific. Most railroads got the same sweetheart deal. For the Union Pacific it figured out to ten square miles of salable land for every mile of track. The land was divided into square-mile sections (640 acres). The government kept the even-numbered sections and the railroad got the odd-numbered. The result was the infamous checkerboard arrangement of section ownership that still disfigures maps of the west. The Union Pacific ran across the center of Wyoming Territory, bisecting the great North American bison herd. Ranchers who bought railroad sections effectively controlled the public or state land that lay between or adjacent to them. Often the buyers illegally enclosed public land with fences. It still happens. Hunters and hikers, photographers, bird-watchers, historians seeking access to public land may find the way closed by illegal gates, barbed wire and No Trespassing signs. Both state and federal government seem powerless to allow access to all public lands.

In the 1862 giveaway the government retained the mineral rights on the railroad sections. Two years later it doubled the land grant appropriation to twenty miles on each side of the tracks and threw in the mineral rights, very pleasing to the Union Pacific which had discovered rich coal deposits in the Wyoming hinterlands. The U.P. freighted in coal miners, and around the mine adits rose the Wyoming towns of Carbon, Hanna, Superior and Rock Springs. Some of the government-retained sections went to the territories and states to finance and support state colleges.

At the time the land was considered to be of low value. There were not many buyers for Wyoming Territory sections of parching winds and hostile Indians. As the railroads were keen to squeeze all possible monies out of the deal, they mortgaged the land grants. Today collectors prize the dozens of old land grant bonds.

In the 1860s Bird Cloud—section 21—was an odd-numbered Union Pacific section. The railroad still owned it in 1908, but in 1909 sold it, along with sections 3, 9, 11, 15 and 23 for eleven thousand dollars and change. The buyer was that poor Vermont farm boy, Thomas A. Cosgriff, who worked his way up to become president of the massive Cosgriff Sheep Company.

The Cosgriff Brothers

Many of the entrepreneurial adventurers who carved up Wyoming were sets of brothers. The Cosgriffs were the sons of an Irish immigrant, John Cosgriff, who settled in Colchester, Vermont (today a suburb of Burlington). Their mother was Mary Barry, a Vermont native. The two older sons were Thomas A. and John B. Cosgriff, educated at Burlington High School, the boys all powerfully ambitious in the get-ahead spirit of their time. The finest expression of that urge to seize and triumph was the poetry of Walt Whitman. The basest expression, detailed in pioneer journals and letters, was the streak of meanness in some pioneers. There are reports of parties on the westward trails who, when forced to abandon their wagons, cut them in half lengthwise, so no one else could use them. Some dog-in-the-manger types chose to make bonfires and burn their abandoned goods in order to prevent others taking them up.

Thomas A. Cosgriff, born in 1854, worked in a mercantile establishment in Burlington. He saved up a little money, and at age twenty-three headed for Denver. There he found work with the May department and dry goods store, founded by David May in Leadville and Denver. May's became Daniels and Fisher, and in the next century controlled many national department stores including Lord & Taylor, Marshall Field's, Filene's. All were swallowed up in 2005 by Federated Department Stores and continue to exist as Macy's, now a chain store in malls across the country.

Thomas Cosgriff, sensing the chance to make something big out of the raw Wyoming Territory, shifted north to Cheyenne in 1882. In Cheyenne he started a general store which did very well. With the profits, he and his brother John B. (Cosgriff Brothers Company), opened stores in nearly fifty Wyoming towns. The Cosgriffs were rivals of J. W. Hugus who graduated from the lucrative job as sutler at Fort Kearney in Nebraska during the Civil War to the sutler's berth at Fort Steele, Wyoming, where he opened the first of a chain of dry goods stores in Wyoming and surrounding states.

Canny Thomas Cosgriff noticed a need for banks and began attaching them to his various stores. Together the brothers bought the First National Bank of Rawlins, started the State Bank of Saratoga, and opened the Cosgriff-Enright company, a wholesale grocery house, in Salt Lake City. In the 1880s the brothers set up the Cosgriff Sheep Company, buying vast acreage in Wyoming, especially land abutting the open range Red Desert, regarded as superior sheep grazing ground. Thomas Cosgriff became one of Wyoming's first self-made multimillionaires and owned banks in Colorado, Utah and Idaho as well as Wyoming. He built a hotel and a railway in Cheyenne, his adopted city. He didn't marry until he was fifty-nine, bad timing as he died three years later in 1916 before his second child, Thomas A. Jr., was born.

His younger brother, John B. Cosgriff, apparently came west with Thomas. Exactly what Thomas did in his employment with the Denver May department store is not clear, but one report has it that John B. (presumably with Thomas) ran a freight line between the Denver and Leadville stores. One source says that John B. had a construction contract to excavate the sites for Denver's famous Tabor Opera House and for the Union Depot. He was a partner with Thomas A. in many ventures—dry goods stores, grocery stores, and beloved of both men, banks. John B. was a director of a dozen banks during his lifetime. He was involved, with one or the other of his brothers, in the lumber business and owned a floral supply house. He even became president of a small railroad. But it is for their sheep operation that the Cosgriffs' name is remembered.

According to contemporary reports the brothers were reticent, frugal and of saving disposition. As they prospered, most of their profits went into more and more sheep which they pastured on Wyoming's Red Desert under the care of a trusted [New?] Mexican foreman, Adiano Apadaca.

Their younger brother James E. joined the two older men around 1890, but soon moved on to Utah. When John B. bought the Commercial National Bank of Salt Lake City he changed its name to the Continental National Bank. James E. became president of this bank, a position he held until he died in 1938, while John B., perhaps something of an éminence gris, served as vice president and one of the directors.

Sheep had been important in the Cosgriffs' home state of Vermont. In 1811 the U.S. consul to Lisbon was William Jarvis, a Boston man who had a farm on the Connecticut River in Weathersfield, Vermont. After Napoleon defeated Spain there was an opportunity to buy stock from the royal Spanish merino flocks, a monopoly that had been carefully protected from foreign buyers until the power shifted. Under the new regime two hundred merino rams and several hundred other sheep went to Jarvis's Weathersfield property. The cold New England winters caused them to grow prodigious fleeces. Jarvis sold purebreds to his neighbors at reasonable prices and Vermont quickly became synonymous with quality wool. By the time the Cosgriff boys were growing up, sheep raising in Vermont was more costly and beginning to give way to dairy farming. It was far cheaper to run sheep in the opening west.

Years after they came to Wyoming the brothers had not forgotten that there was money in wool and they formed their sheep company to take advantage of the territory's thousands of acres of free, open range land. At their most expansive, a Wyoming Wool Growers Association profile says the Cosgriffs ran 125,000 sheep.

In their own way the conservative, long-sighted brothers were as opportunistic as the railroad and mining buccaneers. Thomas Cosgriff in particular had a superior instinct for business and moneymaking through diversification. The brothers bought up the Union Pacific Railroad's odd-numbered sections of land at bargain prices. The railroad, which had not done very well selling arid, sagebrush land to settlers, let the sections go cheaply.

The Cosgriffs developed a reputation for always coming out on top, fencing in government land adjacent to their purchased sections, and overgrazing the national forest lands. They chose promising young men for business partners. They shipped the largest known consignment of Wyoming wool in 1895. In the battles between Wyoming sheepmen and Colorado cattlemen early in the last century, the sheep owners were in the stronger position because of the financial support of the able and savvy Cosgriffs.

A decade into the new century the aging Cosgriffs divided their sheep empire. The Cosgriff Sheep Company property was broken apart, the Cow Creek section going to James E. Cosgriff, the section west of Saratoga sold to John Hartt, one of their young partners. After the estate was settled some twenty thousand acres were left over. L. E. Vivion bought half of that, the land east and south of Rawlins. The remainder was bought by an oil outfit, the Producers and Refiners Company which created the strange little town of Parco (now renamed Sinclair) a few miles east of Rawlins, site of the Sinclair refinery. The land that Vivion bought included the section that became Bird Cloud. It was a descendant of Vivion who sold section 21 to The Nature Conservancy in the 1990s.

L. E. Vivion arrived in Wyoming in the 1880s and worked for Isaac Carson Miller who had emigrated from Denmark in 1864. By 1870 Miller was in Wyoming Territory prospecting for gold, then running a Rawlins saloon. As he settled into the place he began to graze cattle and sheep. By the time Vivion went to work for him, Miller was getting into politics. He was elected sheriff of Carbon County in 1880, and appointed foreman of an extraordinary grand jury overseeing the trial of the notorious bandit-murderer George Parrotte, better known as Big Nose George. Big Nose was sentenced to hang in April 1881, but in late March, when Miller was away from Rawlins on business, the condemned man tried unsuccessfully to escape. A few hours later a vigilante gang took Big Nose forcibly from jail and hanged him from a handy telegraph pole. (Telegraph poles were useful in several ways to early settlers in this treeless country.) The grisly-minded Rawlins doctor, John Osborne, took over the corpse, cut off the top of the skull, and flayed large sections of skin from the body, skin which he ordered tanned and made into a pair of shoes. Eleven years later Dr. Osborne, a Democrat in a staunchly conservative Republican state, somehow got elected governor. He wore his macabre outlaw shoes to the inauguration.

Vivion had learned enough about cows to start a herd and was living the tough ranch life. In a period when fresh vegetables were hard to come by, his ranch grew a garden. The garden was not fenced and, during lambing season in 1892, the ewes of the old Saratoga Valley pioneer, George Ferris, got into the vegetables. The exasperated Vivion got plenty of exercise chasing them out, but the exercise piqued his curiosity. He asked Ferris if there was money in sheep. Ferris said there was indeed, speaking in such a convincing way that Vivion sold his cattle and bought a band of animals from him. Another local man, George Seeley, also bought a band of sheep from Ferris and it was a natural progression for Vivion and Seeley to throw in together. Despite the depression of 1893 they made money and when they broke up six years later each owned four bands of sheep free and clear. A band of sheep is generally assumed to be a thousand animals.

In 1894 Vivion accompanied a Lancashire butcher, Robert Jackson, to the Pick ranch to give advice on the butcher's purchase of steers. They came across a band of ewe sheep belonging to Napoleon "Boney" Earnest, brother of Frank Earnest. Jackson, as payment for Vivion's help in cattle buying, loaned him enough money to purchase those sheep.

Henry Seton-Karr

Henry Seton-Karr held much of the property adjacent to Bird Cloud in the nineteenth century. He discovered world-class hunting and a dubious business opportunity in Wyoming. Although it is not fair to judge him by today's values—historians call this "presentism"—he seems a caricature of the landed gentry in his 1904 *My Sporting Holidays*. Seton-Karr was a Scot and a privileged member of the elite class of wealthy landowners in the British Isles. He wrote his book for "My Brother-Sportsmen of the Anglo-Saxon Race." He was a creature of his times, as we all are. Born in 1853 in India where his colonial service father represented the British Raj, he believed in the inborn rights of patriotic, educated white Britons to rule presumed lesser parts of the world. He saw his class, those representatives of the British Empire, as possessing the inherent freedom to use the entire globe for purposes of monetary gain or pleasure.

He was a sportsman in the way only the wealthiest and most fanatic upper-class shooters of the period from 1870 to the First World War could be. He lived by a sportsman's code and defended the British hunter's "lust to kill the hunted." He was rock-certain that "no race of men possesses this desire more strongly than the Anglo-Saxons of the British Isles . . . an inherited instinct—which civilization cannot eradicate—of a virile and dominant race." His photographs show him in his twenties and thirties as slender, very dapper, and with a large dark mustache. His face was handsome and intense. As the years passed and he spent more time in Parliament than in the forests and fields, he put on weight, and at the time of his dramatic death was fairly hefty.

He always sought out the largest and handsomest animals, and when he was shooting wapiti or red deer or mountain sheep it was the quality of the animal's head that guided his choice of target. And of the head it was the horns he most esteemed, following a complicated horn-and-antler value scale of points. By today's standards he was a game hog: he blithely noted that he and his party once "easily obtained our limit of 800 brace of grouse and blackgame," killed "eighteen stags in ten days' stalking," and on a good day, in the morning caught "a salmon of 12 pounds," while after lunch "three good stags were killed." He seemed unaware that size-focused trophy hunting removed the largest animals from the gene pool, a kind of secondary genetic engineering that favors smaller racks and animals.

Wyoming's first territorial legislature met and passed a feeble law in 1869 to limit the taking of big game, but without provision for enforcement it was writ in water and everywhere flouted—"perhaps one of the most notably ineffective laws of its kind ever passed."[1] Everyone—military men, emigrants, settlers, train passengers, foreign sportsmen—shot animals in truly astounding quantities in the western territories. Seton-Karr was only part of the anything-goes wave of unchecked hunting and fishing.

Many of the early settlers in Wyoming were men who had worked on the Union Pacific Railroad when it pushed through the Territory in 1868, and military men who had served in the Wyoming forts during the Indian wars.[2] One of the perks of these men's hard duties was a certain amount of freedom to hunt and fish. Foreign sportsmen, most of them titled and well-heeled men from the British Isles and Europe with gold-plated bison guns, breech-loading rifles and Purdey shotguns, came with enormous entourages. They hired local guides, bought dozens of wagons, commandeered food and drink, and set out on month-long hunts, for game was not evenly distributed, and could be hard to find. Among these men was Lord George Gore whose immense income came from family land holdings in Ireland. Gore had a bison hunt at Fort Kearney, Nebraska, on his way to Wyoming. Wrote Eugene Ware in his memoir *The Indian War of 1864,* "Lord George Gore came with forty horses, forty servants, forty guns, forty dogs and forty of everything else. He stopped at Fort Kearney and hunted."[3] In Wyoming he arrived at Fort Laramie in 1854 with not quite

1. Douglas Crowe, *The First Century: A Hundred Years of Wildlife Conservation in Wyoming* (Cheyenne: Wyoming Game and Fish Department, 1990), 12.

2. Forts Kearney, Laramie, Halleck, Fred Steele, Bridger and several camps. Quite a few of these men were Irish, and some were "galvanized Yankees," southern prisoners of war who changed sides and joined the U.S. Army.

3. Eugene Ware, *The Indian Wars of 1864* (Topeka, Kan.: Crane & Company, 1911; New York: St. Martin's Press, 1960), ch. 4. Ware profited from Gore's visit, for he was later given a greyhound from a litter that Gore's hunting dogs produced at Fort Kearney.

forty of everything except servants, and lesser numbers of wagons, horses, oxen, dogs and carts. He spent nearly a year hunting. The Earl of Dunraven, Otho Shaw, Moreton Frewen and other wealthy big-game hunters came for the sport and some stayed to play at cattle ranching. Most of them, including Seton-Karr, were robbed blind by the locals. It is not known whether some of the lesser Wyoming ranchers who fattened on the wealthy sportsmen had sprung from landless Irish peasantry whose people had suffered during the famine years of the 1840s, many under the hard yoke of unfeeling British absentee estate owners.

Another British hunter-cattleman of note in the 1880s was Moreton Frewen, an uncle of Winston Churchill, and, despite ideas that ranged from brilliant to farcical, apparently something of an extreme ass. He cut a wide swath in Wyoming, building a log castle north of Casper where he entertained titled and wealthy friends from abroad. Among his friends was Sir Maurice de Bunsen who shot a milk cow under the impression it was a wizened bison, and the Honorable Gilbert Leigh, a member of Parliament, who went out hunting alone and somehow galloped off a cliff to his death. Frewen was loathed by the locals, and after the vicious winter of 1886–1887, was among the cattlemen who went under.

Under the terrific killing pressure the game began to dwindle. The near extinction of some species is an ugly story embedded in our history. Today the human effect on wildlife numbers is a popular subject of scientific study. There is continuing controversy about the cause of the extinction of the woolly mammoth (and other megafauna) around the time humans arrived in North America. Briefly (passing over the complex details of evidence and rival theories), for some it was climate change—a warming period—that modified the ecosystem in ways unfavorable for the vegetation that nurtured mammoths and horses. Evidence from the examination of exhumed dung from these giant animals shows a precipitous drop in the percentages of spores of the fungus *Sporormiella* after 10,800 B.P., indicating a change in climate and a long decline that ended in extinction.[4] Others believe that incoming human predators from the west, expert hunters who took advantage of the animals' naïveté, were major players in the inevitable depletion of mammoth stocks. While a more arid climate may have been the operative factor, it is difficult to ignore how rapidly human hunters can decimate animal populations. We have the example of Wyoming: this was an incredibly rich hunting ground with more than a hundred thousand pronghorn when whites, with their technologically superior weapons for mass killing, came into the country in numbers in the 1860s. By 1910 the nascent Game and Fish Department counted only seven thousand pronghorn antelope in the state.[5]

The beaver had been pretty much trapped out by the 1840s, following the invention of the steel trap in 1823, although the older historical thinking believed the collapse of the beaver trade was linked to a change in men's hat fashions, styles that no longer needed the soft beaver underfur for making glossy felt. In fact, the underfur was no longer available in quantity, for beaver populations had precipitously declined, a hard fact noted by old trappers who remembered the glory days when the animals were so numerous a man could whack them dead with a stick. The great bison herds began to decline around the same time, and although their slaughter by hide hunters was immense, the major collapse had its root in the introduction of

4. Abstract, *Palaeogeography, Palaeoclimatology, Palaeoecology* 237, no. 1 (July 21, 2006); *Fungi* 3, no. 1 (Winter 2010): 5.
    5. http://ahc.uwyo.edu/onlinecollections/exhibits/pronghorn/part4.htm.

cattle diseases with trail herds beginning to make the trek from Texas to Montana and Saskatchewan.[6]

Gradually a distaste for the rampant taking of horns and heads by foreign "sportsmen" grew. In 1875 the Wyoming legislature, perhaps fearing there would be nothing left for *them* to shoot, passed a wildlife law setting a big-game season of August 15 to January 15. The vote was prefaced by Governor John Thayer's reproving report "that one party alone had killed more than 100 elk in the mountains east of the Seminoe district that year" taking "only the teeth and hides, leaving the meat to rot."[7] The legislation also prohibited waste—but only on paper. Hunters did as they pleased.

Seton-Karr and his guns traveled back and forth between the British Isles and North America countless times, always first-class on the great steamers of the day; he was a platinum-card member of the nineteenth-century equivalent of the jet set. In a sense, big-game hunting was more his life's work than were his political career or the duties of running the family estate.

As an Oxford undergraduate he spent the vacation months shooting in Norway, and on his first day on Hitteren island "surprised a golden eagle within 40 yards, as he rose from lunching on a dead sheep. A charge of No. 6 shot up the feathers and brought him wounded to the ground, and we slew him with a stone."[8] On another of those joyful days, he wrote, "I once shot a cock capercaillie, a stag, and a white-tailed eagle

<hr />

6. Dan Flores, "Bison Ecology and Bison Diplomacy: The Southern Plains from 1800–1850," *Journal of American History* 7 (1991): 465–485.

7. Crowe, *First Century,* 15. Unfortunately they neglected to include any enforcement measures which made the law as big a joke as the 1869 exercise in conservation. This was not Seton-Karr's party as he came to Wyoming for the first time in 1877 and his first elk hunt was in August of that year. Henry Seton-Karr, *My Sporting Holidays* (London: Edward Arnold, 1904), 155.

8. Seton-Karr, *My Sporting Holidays,* 3.

with three consecutive shots of a single Henry express rifle, all within the space of ten minutes or less."[9] He might have been content to hunt red deer in Norway and Scotland for the rest of his life but for an accidental glimpse of a tremendous set of antlers.

In 1876, freshly graduated from Oxford, and walking down London's Strand, he saw a formidable set of elk (wapiti) antlers in a gunmaker's shop window. On fire with curiosity he inquired and found the animal had been shot by "Mr. Otho Shaw, who had recently returned from a hunting expedition to Wyoming, whence he had brought some good wapiti heads. From him I obtained an introduction to the western ranchman, Frank Earnest by name, who had accompanied him as hunter and guide."[10] Captain Otho Shaw, the same age and class as Seton-Karr, had just that year acquired Arrowe Hall, a mansion in the Elizabethan style with 450 acres of woods and fields. Shaw's name, along with Henry Seton-Karr's, appears many times in Rowland Ward's *Records of Big Game*.[11]

A few months later twenty-three-year-old Seton-Karr arrived in Rawlins, Wyoming, with his friend Thomas Bate, and the pair made their way to Frank Earnest's ranch "in the valley of the North Platte, about twenty miles south of Fort Steele." Over the next four months scores of elk, grizzly bears, bison, antelope, mule deer and mountain sheep of the Medicine Bow and Sierra Madre ranges, the Rattlesnakes and Bates

9. Ibid., 18.

10. Ibid. 145.

11. Rowland Ward, *Records of Big Game, with Their Distribution, Characteristics, Dimensions, Weights, and Measurements of Horns, Antlers, Tusks and Skins,* 3d ed. (London: Roland Ward, Ltd., 1899). *Records of Big Game* has gone through many editions and reprints. It is instructive to see how many of the largest "true wapiti" heads listed in this book were killed in Wyoming. The state must have been crawling with British shooters in the last quarter of the nineteenth century.

Hole fell before Seton-Karr's rifle. He took few chances with Wyoming grizzly bears, but trapped them and then shot them. A photograph shows the twelve-point elk with fifty-eight-inch antlers he shot in the Medicine Bows. Even so young, he knew he was in a place incredibly rich in wildlife, and looking back over thirty years later when the game had all been shot out and the elk and bighorn herds driven down by domestic sheep and beef cows, he wrote nostalgically:

> At the present time [1904] this country is a huge sheep and cattle ranch. The river-meadows and streams are for the most part wire-fenced. Flock-masters, with their herds and traveling wagons, pass over it to and fro, from summer to winter range, and the wild green pastures of the seventies are now a thing of the past, eaten up, trodden down, and periodically desolated by the thousands of domestic sheep that have largely added to the wealth of Wyoming, but have, on the other hand, ruined a large part of the state . . . as a game-preserve and a hunting-ground. . . . But in the days of which I write Wyoming was a hunter's paradise.[12]

He came back to Carbon County and the North Platte again and again, first to hunt and fish and, finally, when the bison were gone and most of the biggest heads hung on the walls of estates in the British Isles, to vaguely oversee the cattle ranch that became his in 1883.

Frank and Bonaparte "Boney" Earnest were two Canadian brothers who had come from Toronto to Wyoming Territory to trap, guide and fight in the Indian wars. They eventually took up cattle ranching. Seton-Karr liked and trusted Frank

12. Seton-Karr, *My Sporting Holidays,* 151.

Earnest but apparently had suspicions about Boney Earnest's probity. After seven years of hunting acquaintance, Seton-Karr bought the Earnest ranch, renamed it Sand Creek Land and Cattle Company, and hired Frank as manager. Together they purchased two thousand Utah cows to run on the open range. The ranch pastures extended seventy miles north from the North Platte River, the first of the big ranches in this part of Wyoming. The brand was in the form of a pick, and no one called the ranch the Sand Creek outfit—it was known to all by the brand, the Pick Ranch. Today the old log ranch house still stands, where our neighbor Ken Olson and his family lived for years before selling to the TA Ranch, then bordering Bird Cloud on the northwest, in 2006. The Seton-Karr house, as well as much of the ranch property, currently belong to the TA Ranch, owned by Campbell's Foods and its subsidiary, Pace hot sauce. This ranch currently abuts Bird Cloud on two sides.

Henry Seton-Karr also had investment interests in the XIT, the giant ranch of the Texas Panhandle first known as the Capitol Ranch. Chicago businessmen had made a deal with the Texas legislature that they, the businessmen, would supply the money for the new capitol building after the original burned down, in return for 3 million acres of the unsettled panhandle region. The Capitol Freehold Land and Investment Company of London attracted wealthy investors, including Seton-Karr and the Earl of Aberdeen. It was an agreeable bargain for both parties, and the Capitol became known as the XIT after Ab Blocker, who drove the first thousands of cattle onto the property, drew a brand that supposedly could not be altered, in the dust with his boot heel. The XIT was the largest cattle ranch in the world, and its size likely appealed to that pursuer of gigantism, Seton-Karr. Later he was tangentially linked to the other very large ranch of the Texas Panhandle, the Matador.

The Pick Ranch, like other big Wyoming spreads with absentee owners, suffered loss and depredations. Wrote Seton-Karr, "It was extraordinary how herds of range cattle, bought often on book-count, melted away in the course of a few years from off the wild unfenced prairies and foot-hills of Montana, Wyoming and Colorado."[13]

"Book count" was one of the most stupid practices in cattle ranching during the last quarter of the nineteenth century. The owner made an estimate—often just a wild guess—of the number of cows in his herds and wrote it down in a notebook. Later, if he sold a herd, the gentlemen's agreement figures in the book were taken as reality. Tales abound of cheating, lying, imaginative cattlemen selling paper cows that did not exist. Eventually the light came on and buyers and bankers realized that an actual count was necessary. Seton-Karr admitted that bad winters and book counts were partially responsible "for the disappearance of good English dollars that have jumped into western pockets and have since given little or no return."[14] There was another reason for the lack of income: cattle rustling.

The titled Scotsman tried to make light of the unpleasant fact that Pick cows seemed to decrease in number instead of multiplying. He wrote in an amused tone that "many western owners possessed . . . ragged old Texas cows of an extraordinary fecundity, even in seasons when the big outfit of the neighborhood had had, maybe, a very poor branding season. Two celebrated cows . . . on Sand Creek, belonging to an old native rancher of my acquaintance and his wife, were known in two years to have ostensibly produced no less than fifty-two calves." In the best Wyoming style of local justice, the

13. Seton-Karr, *My Sporting Holidays,* 284.
14. Ibid.

"old rancher and his wife were found hanging to a convenient cottonwood-tree . . . one fine morning." Seton-Karr declares sanctimoniously that the perpetrators were unknown, but slyly adds that among those rumored to be responsible, was a candidate for the state legislature.[15] In a later chapter Seton-Karr mentions that Boney Earnest was running for election to the legislature.

This story sounds suspiciously like a tale based on the 1889 vigilante hanging of the homesteader Jim Averell and nearby Ella Watson, the latter believed to have traded sexual favors to cowboys in return for mavericks. (She was called Cattle Kate by a Chicago newspaperman.) Some historians see the double hanging as an early chapter in the Johnson County War. This big-rancher-versus-little-homesteader "war" became the plot basis for countless western movies. As Miss Watson was, according to the historian T. A. Larson, "the only woman ever hanged in Wyoming, legally or illegally," Seton-Karr's loose account was probably patched together through hearsay and imagination; he undoubtedly dined out on it for years. Larson names the perpetrators as "A. J. Bothwell, Tom Sun, John Durbin, R. M. Galbraith, Bob Connor, E. McLain and an unknown man."[16] Seton-Karr's account of the Johnson County War is also suspect, as he confuses the town of Buffalo with Casper, and, unlike most historians, says the hired Texas gunmen were Texas Rangers. It is possible he knew something we don't from his XIT connections in the Texas Panhandle, but nothing in the literature suggests the Rangers were the mysterious hired Texas gunmen.

There was a rustler closer to home. One of the Pick Ranch

15. Seton-Karr, *My Sporting Holidays,* 284–285, 322.
16. T. A. Larson, *History of Wyoming,* 2d ed. (Lincoln: University of Nebraska Press, 1965, 1978), 269.

cowboys was Charley Smith, "a long-legged, powerful rider of the ideal cowboy type." The Pick foreman was Chico, a fine roper. One day Chico asked Frank Earnest and Seton-Karr if he could fire any cowboy he wanted. They, somewhat puzzled, said yes. Chico explained that he thought Charley Smith was too handy with a rope. Local talk indicated that Smith was in league with a Rawlins butcher, Al Hurt, whose new "flatiron" brand appeared tailor-made to absorb the "pick" with only a few alterations.

It was September and the fall roundup was at hand. While Chico and the cowhands gathered the three- and four-year-olds "destined to provide dividends for shareholders in the old country 5,000 miles away," Seton-Karr and a party of friends would be on a month-long hunt in the Medicine Bow range. They arranged that cowboys and hunters would meet up "at the far side of the range." It did not work out that way.

The second night in the hunting camp, one of the Pick crew, Jack Savage, galloped in with the news that Charley Smith had killed Chico after Chico fired him. When Smith started to retaliate, Chico shot at him. Smith's thick-rolled neckerchief saved his life. Chico wasn't so lucky, and died that night with—according to Seton-Karr—the pathetic last words, "Boys, I die for the Pick." He is supposedly buried in a Rawlins cemetery. Seton-Karr was annoyed, for he and his hunting companions had to give up their hunt and gather cows for the next three weeks; the shareholders in Scotland and England were waiting for their dividends. Charley Smith came to a bad end a few years later, plugged by a rancher who knew the man had been rustling his stock.[17]

In late May 1914, the sixty-one-year-old Seton-Karr, still

17. Seton-Karr, *My Sporting Holidays,* 287–294.

fit from a lifetime of athletic adventures, enjoyed a successful climbing holiday in British Columbia and was on his way
back to London. In Québec City he boarded the S.S. *Empress
of Ireland,* a Canadian Pacific Railway luxury ocean liner on
which he had his usual first-class accommodations. The ship,
with fifteen hundred passengers, and fitted with sufficient lifeboats after the tragedy of the *Titanic* two years before, sailed
in late afternoon, heading east down the St. Lawrence Sea-
way. An hour and a half after midnight the pilot left the ship at
Rimouski and the *Empress* steamed toward the open Atlantic.
Very soon after the pilot left, Captain Henry George Kendall,
on his first trip with the *Empress,* saw a low-lying collier coming up the river. The coal carrier, S.S. *Storstad,* from Sydney,
Nova Scotia, was heavily laden. Exactly what happened next is
still not clear, as heavy spring fog blanked out everything and
the accounts given at the later investigation varied. The *Storstad*
somehow rammed the *Empress* amidships. The beautiful liner
sank in fourteen minutes. So swiftly did she go down there was
not enough time to launch more than a few lifeboats. Among
the 1,012 people who lost their lives was Henry Seton-Karr,
but a *New York Times* report on the tragedy depicted him as a
hero who gave his life jacket to a man who had none, saying
confidently that he would get another. He didn't.

Over the next century Bird Cloud was used as pasture for
sheep, for cows, for horses, for deer. The native shrubs and
grasses disappeared under the decades of grazing assault. By
the time we bought the property in 2003 most of the native
grasses were gone, only a few winged saltbush shrubs existed.
Cheatgrass had moved in along with leafy spurge, Canada
thistle and whitetop, all noxious weeds. There were no cottonwood seedlings, only older trees, most in poor condition,
racked by storm and cows rubbing against them.

We began a program of rehabilitation, trying to eradicate the cheatgrass, then sowing inland salt grass on its former ground. As soon as the fencing was complete marauding cows were barred from the property. The simple step of removing grazing pressure encouraged cottonwood sprouts to spring up by the thousand. We planted trees, willows, encouraged the saltbush which suddenly began to appear. The James Gang planted some beautiful lodgepole pines from Idaho, but we discovered these were like candy to porcupines who came in the winter nights and reduced the trees to skeletons. Any new plant was immediately attacked by deer and porcupine. We should have planted only local trees, such as juniper and cedar.

Wildlife has cautiously moved onto the property, several elk now spending the winter near Jack Creek. Owls enjoy the bosque at the east end. Skunks wander around, eating insects and bothering no one. A sage grouse restoration project with Wyoming Game and Fish is in the talking stage; it would provide water and shade for these birds. The land has generously responded to the slightest care. I wish I had a lifetime to see it recover.

CHAPTER 9

"... all beaded, all earringed, wing feather bowstring sided ..."[1]

chert corner-notch point fractured. Sides retouched. Excellent flaking. Likely Rose Springs projectile point, common between 300 and 1500 A.D.

desert side notch w. re-use area suggesting re-sharpening for use as a drill. Originally an arrowhead likely hafted on a reed or thin service-berry branch.

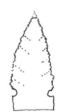

pink quartz side-notched projectile point w. broken tip. Falling Cow site. 2007

Robert Louis Stevenson, on his 1879 journey across this continent, wrote a wonderful line about New York: "Old, red Manhattan lies, like an Indian arrowhead under a steam factory, below New York."[2] So, too, does old red Wyoming lie under

1. Donald M. Bahr, "Thin Leather's Oration," in *Pima and Papago Ritual Oratory: A Study of Three Texts* (San Francisco: Indian Historian Press, 1975), 45.
2. Robert Louis Stevenson, *Across the Plains* (London: Chatto and Windus, 1892), 12.

this trammeled ground. According to some estimates, people have lived here for more than ten thousand years.

After Bird Cloud was finished and I was living in the house I found that the Euro-American division of time into five-day workweeks and two-day weekends crumbled away. I became more intensely aware of the seasons, animal movements, plant behavior and I could imagine the different shape of time in the Indian world by thinking, for example, of the Papago-Pima "calendar" made accessible to me through poetic translations of ritual oratory. The anthropologists Ruth M. Underhill and Donald M. Bahr, in *Rainhouse and Ocean,* explained that the important times are not some arbitrary "beginning of the year" date, but the solstices, the longest day (June 21) and shortest day (December 21). Their year fell into approximately three seasons, each with four moons. Instead of a catalog of months there were certain important moons with ritual ceremonies attached to them, as the winter solstice "backbone moon" when days and nights were equal in length and it was fitting to tell the creation story. A second important time was the "summer wine feast" preceded by the "Saguaro ripe moon" when the important picking of saguaro fruits occurred. Then came the "rainy moon" of summer clouds and precipitation followed by the "dry grass moon." The fermentation of the fruits, the drinking of the wine, feasts and traditional oratory followed this lunar progression and went on to the "surviving moon" honoring plants that were not felled by the first frosts. The last month in their year was the "black seed moon" preceding the ripening of the saguaro cactus fruits. I wondered if a similar calendar had guided the ancient people living around Bird Cloud. It is not knowable. It all must be imagined.

Scholarly research over the past decades has massively

changed our ideas of what the western North American Indian world and its inhabitants were like before the incursion of white people. Instead of a few wandering tribes in a vast, untamed wilderness, which is what I learned as a child, there was a large population of many, many tribes who practiced advanced agriculture and deliberate control of wild animals, made landscape modifications through fire and irrigation, built a variety of houses and shelters, in the southwest erected enormous building complexes and supported sophisticated religions and mythologies.

The ecological historian James C. Malin, on the subject of whether or not Indians lived in pure harmony with the natural world, inflicting no change or scars on the land, wrote: "The conventional or traditional concept of the state of nature must be abandoned—that mythical idealized condition, in which natural forces, biological and physical, were supposed to exist in a state of virtual equilibrium, undisturbed by man. The role of aboriginal man within the ecosystem must be recognized as a major ecological fact."[3] In short, there was no sustained "balance" of nature, just ongoing, incremental, shifting change in which humans played a central role.

Trying to understand Wyoming's landscape where I could see the remains of Indian trails, stone flakes from their toolmaking, the tools themselves, images scratched into the dark desert varnish of rock faces, cairns and fire pits forced recognition: where there are humans there is always ecological change. In the southwest we are stunned by the huge abandoned build-

3. J. C. Malin, "Soil, Animal, and Plant Relations of the Grassland, Historically Reconsidered," *Scientific Monthly* 75 (1953), 207–220, cited in Gordon G. Whitney, *From Coastal Wilderness to Fruited Plain: A History of Environmental Change in Temperate North America from 1500 to the Present* (Cambridge: Cambridge University Press, 1994), 98.

ings of Chaco, Canyon de Chelly, Mesa Verde, Comb Ridge and the Mogollon Rim. Any visitor immediately wonders, What happened here? Who built these fantastic structures? In Wyoming and Utah the extraordinary rock art of the Fremont people, about whom little is known, urges the same questions.

The general statement is sometimes made that North American Indians had not reached the point where their numbers exceeded natural resources when Europeans arrived. But over-population as well as the severe droughts that struck the southwest in the twelfth and thirteenth centuries may have greatly contributed to the emptying of the large cultural center of Chaco in north-central New Mexico. Aridity may also have forced out the Fremont people in Utah and Wyoming. Climate studies for the past two millennia show extreme droughts lasting as long as fifty years hit the southwest roughly every five centuries. Twenty-year droughts came roughly every 275 years.[4] We are beginning to learn a little about the effects of climate change on species, including our own.

The ancestral people who built Mesa Verde's and Chaco's kivas and great houses with hundreds of rooms likely did not disappear in some supernatural mystery, the stuff of bad "science" television. We wonder today how they could leave these magnificent buildings, but without water the most exquisite palace is worthless. When their world began to shrivel they apparently fought and killed each other, perhaps over tiny water seeps. As their descendants know, these disparate people eventually evolved into today's Hopi and regional Pueblo populations who laugh at the myth of a mysterious ancestral disappearance.

4. R. Gwinn Vivian and Bruce Hilpert, *The Chaco Handbook* (Salt Lake City: University of Utah Press, 2002), 95.

American Indians invented more than twenty kinds of housing—wigwams, tipis, brush huts, plank houses, pueblos, grass houses and pit houses. The plains and mountain tribes did not build permanent structures such as the great stone and cliff houses of the southwest. In the Archaic period, pit houses, which took advantage of passive solar sites, were warmer in winter and cooler in summer than aboveground structures. Essentially these were rectangular or circular holes dug in the earth with deeper fire pits, roofed with frameworks of willows and brush, then covered with hides and perhaps more soil. Because they were fixed, they may indicate a population of relatively sedentary people. Later, with the coming of the horse, the portable tipi better suited the swiftly moving tribes that flowed across the landscape like the meltwater from winter snows.

Prehistoric Indians (and all people who live by hunting and gathering) had bone-deep knowledge of their enormous and seasonally elastic habitat. Local animals and people recognized one another, a kind of familiar awareness where species understood each other's body language and behavior to a considerable extent. If there is one word that describes western Indians before whites came it is "flexible." The most important trait in humans is adaptability, the power to change and exploit difficult situations. Somewhere deep behind the gauzy layers of the past this attribute helped humans develop the ingenious mind that characterizes the species.

The Indian world was diversely layered. The sky and its inhabitant birds and stars made the overarching highest layer. On the horizon, mountain ranges, constantly in sight, were the place for the plains tribes to cut poles for travois and lodge, and to find the best wood for bows. The Sierra Madre (the Utes' Shining Mountains) on Bird Cloud's south hori-

zon had the reputation among plains tribes of being mysterious and dangerous to outsiders. Only the Utes knew the
passes and trails of their stronghold. The rock maze canyon
lands, cliffs and mesas of the southwest, remote and nearly
inaccessible, offered sanctuary to beleaguered and shifting
tribal groups.[5]

Cottonwoods along the rivers made the tallest vegetative
layer, and on the surrounding prairies grew shoulder-high
sage and greasewood, punctuated by the bunchgrasses close
to the ground. Below the earth were the tunnels of plowing
and burrowing badgers, prairie dogs, black-footed ferrets,
mice, foxes, skunks, marmots, thirteen-striped chipmunks
and ground squirrels, their subterranean work loosening and
aerating the soil, allowing rainfall and snowmelt to recharge
the water table below. Both humans and animals dug and ate
a vast variety of tubers and roots. Both humans and animals
scavenged each others' kills. The humans followed migratory
animals, understood the growth stages of plants, perhaps coming to the wetlands below Bird Cloud's cliff to gather cattail
shoots and later, the golden pollen, to the slopes at the top to
dig and collect sego lily root, biscuit-root, yucca root, to gather
wild grains where the Indian ricegrass still grows in the blow
sand on the north side of the property. Slough grass was used as
thatching, sweetgrass and sage were burned in ceremonial ritu-
als. The tips of porcupine grass (*Stipa spartea*) could be bound

---

5. We know little about those invisible movements of people over thousands
of years. Craig Childs tells in his *House of Rain: Tracking a Vanished Civilization
Across the American Southwest,* (New York: Little, Brown and Co., 2007), how he
has spent most of his life walking and puzzling out the trails of ancestral pueblo
people through ruins, broken pottery, water sources and artifacts and conversations with archaeologists and historians. He has on-the-ground knowledge of
the sometimes terrifyingly high and remote places these people lived that few
of us will ever see.

together and the awns burned off to make small, stiff-bristled hairbrushes.[6] We know that trade—in chert, obsidian, seeds, plants, special woods for bows and arrows, food, shells, furs and hides, and from the distant tallgrass prairie, red clay stone catlinite for medicine pipes—was vigorous and extensive even before the horse arrived.

That world not only was arranged in multiple layers, each layer with its own set of meanings and uses, but flowed outward and inward in expansive, large regions, very differently ordered than the white man's small-space cadastral categories of acre, plot and township. It was a world curved rather than rectilinear, outlined by streams, particular habitats, trails and geophysical landmarks. Running through everything these people thought or knew, like the vast root systems of grasses that extend deep beneath the surface, as intricate as the lacework of billions of spiderwebs, were spiritual filaments that guided behavior and nourished rich mythologies. We today can barely comprehend the interconnectedness of their observations of the natural world, their ideas and lives.

Custer's Crow scout, Curley, a survivor of the Battle of Greasy Grass, spoke in council in 1907 when pressure was on to sell part of the Crow Reservation to outsiders. He said, "The soil you see is not ordinary soil. It is the dust of the blood of the flesh and bones of our ancestors. We fought and bled and died to keep other Indians from taking it and fought and bled and died, helping the whites. You will have to dig through the surface before you can find the earth, as the upper portion is Crow. The land as it is, is my blood, and my dead; it is conse-

6. Melvin R. Gilmore, *Uses of Plants by the Indians of the Missouri River Region* (Lincoln: University of Nebraska Press, 1977, 2004), 14–16; *Grassland Plants of South Dakota and the Great Northern Plains,* South Dakota Agricultural Experiment Station bulletin B566 (Brookings, South Dakota, 1999).

crated, and I don't want to give up any portion of it."[7] White people never understood this. They thought buying land made it theirs. To the Indian selling land was a bizarre and impossible idea—how could one sell what belonged to all, the repository of family and tribal ancestors, the source of life? What might Curley think today when corporations aggressively take control of and commodify running water that for all of human and animal history has been as free as sunlight and air?

Emigrant traffic of the 1840s and '50s cut through major Indian hunting grounds and alarmed and angered the Indians because the white incursion frightened away the game and threatened tribal existence. Again and again the Indians raised this point in the endless treaty negotiations with the U.S. government. Treaties were the grossly flawed instruments for transferring Indian lands to the United States. But treaties could not and did not work because of the vastly different cultural perceptions of the opposing parties.

Indians were masters of oratory. In council they spoke at great length, and objectors to the proposed business voiced their concerns. The discussions continued—for hours, for days—until they reached consensus, possible only when all objections had ceased. In treaty council with whites the Indians put forward their objections to the proposals before them, usually with rich similes drawn from the natural world. The white men listened through a translator, and generally failed to make an oratorical response, their silence interpreted by the Indians as recognition of and acquiescence to Indian objections. But when the Indians signed the treaties their objections were not incorporated in the text. Even worse, signing

7. Frances Carrington, *My Army Life and the Fort Phil Kearny Massacre* (Denver: Pruett Press, 1990), 314, cited in John D. McDermott, *A Guide to the Indian Wars of the West* (Lincoln: University of Nebraska Press, 1998), 2.

was meaningless as the U.S. Senate had the post facto power to change the treaty provisions. White men never understood the Indian way of consensus and insisted on dealing with a tribal leader or "chief," another concept alien to Indians who learned to greatly distrust the lying, devious white men whose treaties were worthless. On the other side, most whites regarded Indian oratory as a kind of obstructionist filibustering, boring harangues, though some admired them and saw them as akin to classical Roman oratory.[8]

There was, in the eighteenth and nineteenth centuries in the United States, as the tribes were defeated, moved, killed and warehoused, a widespread belief that these were doomed people on the way to extinction. Part of this belief came from the oratory wherein the Indian speaker would describe the wrongs and injustices done them by the whites in poetic and mournful language to paint a picture of oppression and decimation. Newspaper misinterpretations of these speeches usually showed the Indians as poetically and mournfully bowing to their own inevitable demise.[9]

Lawrence Counselman Wroth (1884–1970), the librarian of the John Carter Brown library at Brown University, believed that nineteenth-century "supporters of American literary inde-

8. The excellent word "filibuster" sprouted from the Dutch word for pirate—*vrijbuiter*—a freebooter seeking prizes. Other languages borrowed the word. The Spanish converted it to *filibustero*. From the Spanish it entered American English in the nineteenth century as adventurers tried to seize personal kingdoms in Latin America. These rogue efforts were discussed at length in the U.S. Senate, and comparisons were not lost there. (The tactic had been used by the Roman senator Cato the Young.) Uncontrolled talkers began to be described as "filibustering." Gradually the word took on the meaning of causing a delaying action by taking advantage of the senatorial right to speak interminably on any subject without restriction.

9. A valuable study of Indian oratory, with many examples, is William M. Clements, *Oratory in Native North America* (Tucson: University of Arizona Press, 2002).

pendence . . . could . . . suggest that Indian speech making would provide some of the basis for a distinctive American heritage of letters."[10] There are not many champions of this view that Indian oratory was the country's first indigenous literature, but it is an observation that deserves some respect.

It didn't help the Indians' situation that one of the most rotten and corrupt systems of graft and profit taking in American history characterized the so-called Indian Ring after the Civil War, a hierarchy extending from high government officials and politicians down to fort sutlers, traders and Indian agents whose rapacity and venal grasping beggar description. Criminal stealage extended to such businesses as the railroads, the Wells Fargo freight line, private citizens and settlers. The criminal behavior tainted the Territorial history of Wyoming.[11]

Indian populations were not randomly mobile, although the picture of aimless wandering is still embedded in white people's minds. Travel and movement into new frontiers and territories, climate change and herd migrations and breakups of groups caused an ebb and flow in clans and tribes, in languages and mythologies so complex it is nearly impossible to link tribes with definite territories. Matching languages and words give clues, and this is how we know, for example, that one group left the northern Shoshone and went to the southwest where they metamorphosed into the Comanche. We don't know what kinds of discussions, arguments or feelings went into these separations.

We rely largely on nineteenth-century sources to give us hints of which tribes were where. Albert Gallatin's 1836 "Map

10. Clements, *Oratory,* citing Wroth in his essay in *Literature of the American Indians: Views and Interpretations,* ed. Abraham Chapman (New York: New American Library, 1975).

11. See McDermott, *Guide.*

of the Indian Tribes of North America" shows that in the larger area north of the Saratoga Valley were Blackfeet, Crow, Cheyenne, Sioux, Shoshone.[12] The Belgian "Black Robe" Father Pierre-Jean De Smet, who spent many years among the Indians of the Great Plains and Rocky Mountains, made an important map for the 1851 Fort Laramie Treaty.[13] For Bird Cloud's area he named Crow, Utah Indians, Arapaho, Cheyenne and, to the east in present-day Nebraska, the Sioux. The Shoshone were farther northwest. Judging from local settler and traveler sources, several tribes used the Saratoga Valley—Bird Cloud is at the northern end of the valley—as a prime hunting ground and for the curative hot springs now owned by the town of Saratoga. Local sources name Cheyenne, Arapaho, Sioux, Snakes (Shoshone) and Crow as the tribes that were in the region.[14] The valley was a borderland place used by both plains tribes and mountain people. The mountain people—Utes—came into the valley to hunt and perhaps fight. For millennia Elk Mountain (altitude 11,156 feet), to the northeast of Bird Cloud, has been the great regional landmark, and several sources claim the lands around this mountain were a favored site for annual warfare.

But were these confrontations "fights to the death" as historical lore has it? Several local engagements were described

---

12. "Map of the Indian Tribes of North America," drawn in 1836 by Albert Gallatin, New York Public Library, reproduced in Paul Cohen, *Mapping the West: America's Westward Movement 1524–1890* (New York: Rizzoli, 2002), 114–115.

13. Carl Wheat, *Mapping the Trans-Mississippi West 1540–1861,* vol. 3, *The Mexican War to the Boundary Survey 1846–1854* (San Francisco: Institute of Historical Cartography, 1959), 129 ff. ". . . a really great map drawn by Father de Smet in 1851 for the Indian Bureau. It is a large and detailed map showing all the Indian Tribes from the Missouri River to the junction of the Snake and Columbia rivers, and from the Canadian border to the southern border of New Mexico."

14. Gay Day Alcorn, *Tough Country: The History of the Saratoga and Encampment Valley 1825–1895* (Saratoga, Wyo.: Legacy Press, 1984), 14, 28, 29–38, 49, 62.

by old settlers. The earliest so-called battle was a reference to Charles Fremont's second expedition in 1843–1844 through the Rocky Mountains. By early August the party was on the Laramie plain heading for the Medicine Bow range after an encounter with "a war party of Sioux and Cheyenne Indians about thirty strong."[15] On August 2 they camped on Medicine Bow River near Elk Mountain, about thirty miles from Bird Cloud. They went through the pass south of the mountain and killed a bison in the Saratoga Valley. As they were drying the bison meat, "the camp was thrown into a sudden tumult by a charge from about 70 mounted Indians . . . a war party of Arapaho and Cheyenne . . . [who] informed us that they had charged upon the camp under the belief that we were hostile Indians, and had discovered their mistake only at the moment of attack."[16] This was a nonviolent encounter rather than a battle, but old settlers' tales hashing and rehashing earlier events puffed it up.

The Saratoga historian Gay Day Alcorn stated that the Saratoga Valley was "a treasured hunting ground" where lookouts on the top of Old Baldy mountain surveying the valley sent messages directing the hunters to the herds.[17] The general region around the hot springs was regarded as neutral territory, but "the springs was surrounded by a fierce war ground in which the Sioux, Cheyenne, Snakes, Crow, Arapaho, and Utes battled to the death." By the 1850s and '60s the "Utes seem to have become the foremost tribe."[18] Alcorn describes "one of the last full-scale Indian battles . . . in the late 1860's" in which

15. *Expeditions of John Charles Frémont,* ed. Donald Jackson and Mary Lee Spence (Urbana: University of Illinois Press, 1970), 1:457.
16. Ibid., 1:462.
17. Alcorn, *Tough Country,* 62.
18. Ibid.

five hundred Sioux and fifteen hundred Utes fought east of Bird Cloud and east of present-day Saratoga. "The Utes completely decimated the Sioux in the Pass Creek Basin. Pioneer forefathers recalled that wagon loads of skeletons were everywhere in that section."

One of the pioneer forefathers referenced was Taylor Pennock who enlisted in the 16th Regiment of the Illinois Volunteer Cavalry in 1862 and traded with the Pawnee near Fort Kearney, Nebraska, after the war. He found civilian life too tame and came west to Wyoming, got a government contract to supply ten thousand telegraph poles, batted around a few years, went back to Illinois and didn't like it, returned to Wyoming Territory, shot elk for the railroad tie-hack camp, trapped beaver, mined gold, tended bar, built a hotel that burned down, guided hunting trips and hauled supplies to the tie-hack camps. His centers of operation were Fort Steele, about thirty miles northwest of Bird Cloud as the crow flies, and the nascent settlement of Saratoga. Pennock got the story of the big Ute-Sioux fight from a Mr. Wilcox—perhaps the cowboy named Wilcox who worked for the big L7—who heard it from Tom Sun, a very tough local rancher from Vermont by way of Québec where he had been Tom Soleil.[19]

These accounts of pitched battles and hundreds of corpses have entered the local mythology and the history books but should be taken with a handful of salt. Terrific battles and decimation of the enemy, wholesale slaughter and wagonloads of corpses were not the Indian style of warfare according to hun-

19. "Recollections of Taylor Pennock as Dictated to Mr. I. R. Conniss, Saratoga, Wyoming, April, 1927," *Annals of Wyoming* 6, nos. 1–2 (July–October 1929): 199–212. Not all of the old settlers were as dependable in their accounts of the past as Pennock. James M. Sherrod's account of *his* life was disputed by other old-timers. See *Annals of Wyoming* 4, no. 3 (January 1927): 325 ff. for Sherrod's tales.

dreds of sources from the period. Although war was extraordinarily important to Indian men, individual achievement and valor, not killing, was the goal. Wrote military historian John D. McDermott, "War was absolutely necessary for the men. Without recognized competence in it, a man could not expect to gain prestige or a mate. Historians generally group Indian reasons for going to war into four categories: to acquire horses, to protect themselves and their territory from intruders, to exact revenge, and to gain respect."[20] Among the Sioux, eagle feathers represented enemies killed. A greater proof of courage than killing was counting coup—physically touching, or scalping an enemy, striking a dead enemy, or riding directly and alone into an enemy camp and touching a lodge with one's weapon. Red Cloud claimed to have counted coup eighty times.

Jack Creek comes down from the Sierra Madre and flows into the North Platte at Bird Cloud. It is a curious source of pleasure to stand on the bridge and look up at the snowfield in the distant mountains and know that is where the stream begins. This creek was named for the Ute warrior Chief Jack, a.k.a. Ute Jack. His Indian name was Nicaagat (which means "green leaf" or "one with earring" according to various sources). Taylor Pennock said there were no ranches in the Saratoga Valley when he arrived in the 1870s. "The Utes used to come into the valley every spring and fall to hunt for meat but didn't molest us. There were two camps of the Utes—one Ute camp was on Jack Creek and was under Chief Jack, after whom Jack Creek is named."[21]

As a child Ute Jack was sold by slave traders to a Salt Lake

20. McDermott, *Guide*.
21. *Annals of Wyoming* 6, nos. 1–2 (July–October 1929): 199ff. This may be the area a mile west of Bird Cloud where scores of tipi rings are still visible, one notably smaller than the others.

City Mormon family where he learned English before eventually escaping.[22] He occasionally served as an interpreter for the
U.S. military, had been to Washington and had a presidential
medal. He played a major role in the so-called Meeker Massacre. The sanctimonious Fourierist Nathan Meeker, who wrote
for Horace Greeley's *New York Herald Tribune,* was deeply
involved in settling Greeley, Colorado, which he was determined to make into a utopian colony. He borrowed money
from Horace Greeley to buy up as much land as he could at
the site of the future Eden. Unfortunately Greeley died soon
after the project started and his heirs called in Meeker's note.
Forced to sell his lately acquired lands for almost nothing
Meeker was left with a sizable debt and had to find a job. In
1878 he wangled the post of superintendent of the White River
Indian Agency in a cold, remote valley, a region that interested white miners. Three bands of Utes were assigned to this
agency. The aim of the government at this time was to convert
all Indians into farmers. Even John Wesley Powell who eventually headed up the new Bureau of Ethnology thought hunters could be made into farmers. He wrote, "The sooner this
country is entered by white people and the game destroyed so
that the Indians will be compelled to gain subsistence by some
other means than hunting, the better it will be for them."[23]

Meeker, still saturated with Fourierist ideals, took up the
challenge of making the horse-loving warrior-hunter Utes into
happy farmers. Meeker believed that if he got rid of their horses
the Utes would be more tractable. In his zeal, he ordered their
best horse pasture and racetrack plowed and planted to corn.
This did not go down well. Ute Jack was the war chief for the

22. Peter R. Decker, *The Utes Must Go: American Expansion and the Removal of a
People* (Golden, Colo.: Fulcrum Publishing, 2004), 101.
23. Decker, *The Utes Must Go,* 99.

bands and had many followers, though the whites regarded two other Indians as the primary chiefs. Trouble escalated and Meeker began to write untruthful letters to his superiors claiming that he had been assaulted by the Indians, that they were setting forest fires. Eventually the inexperienced Major Thomas Thornburgh, the commanding officer at Fort Fred Steele in Wyoming, got orders to proceed to the agency with his men. Through messages to and from Meeker it was agreed that Thornburgh, guided by the Rawlins livery stable owner Charles Rankin, would meet Meeker at Milk Creek with no more than five men to discuss the situation but would not cross the creek. Milk Creek marked the reservation boundary. The Utes, who had not fought the United States to that date, threatened war if troops came across the boundary creek.

As Thornburgh and his men advanced, Ute Jack and the Indians were waiting on a vantage point to see if the major followed the rules. In violation of the agreement the troops crossed Milk Creek. A shot was fired by someone unknown and the battle was on. One of the first to die was Major Thornburgh. When Ute Jack saw Thornburgh fall he also knew what the inevitable future of the Utes would be; he left the battle. A messenger was killed; Meeker, back at the agency settlement, was killed. Soldiers and Indians crashed down from their saddles. Rankin made a daring ride for help which eventually came and saved Thornburgh's troops from annihilation. The Utes were driven west to Utah and miners and settlers rushed onto their White River reservation land.

Ute Jack had a dreadful end. A newspaper story of the period began with the gross sentence "Only once in history of the Wyoming country is it recorded that a single Indian was dignified by being made the sole target for a cannon." Ute Jack, who had taken refuge in a tipi on the Shoshone reservation at

Fort Washakie and was betrayed by an army spy, was that target. The *Laramie Sentinel* turned this outrage into high humor with a mock obituary celebrating the scattering of his brains "over four acres of sagebrush" and adding, "His body will lie in state in a cigar box, until the time . . . he will be interred with . . . a corn planter."[24]

The thriving, rich civilizations and cultures of North and South America collapsed under the ravages of imported diseases against which indigenous people had no built-up immunities. Until the 1960s white historians seemed unaware that swaths of disease had killed vast Indian numbers. In the late nineteenth century, white travelers in the American west described Indians as dirty, primitive, dull-eyed and listless. They were seeing (but not comprehending) the sick, demoralized, rootless remnants of once-healthy, intelligent, vigorous people whose languages and cultures had been gutted by the wildfires of smallpox and other European diseases. Many early Wyoming settlers were pleased when large numbers of Indians died. A particularly repugnant passage from an article, "The Greatest Trout-Fishing Town in the World," by C. E. Van Loan in the July 1910 issue of *The Outing Magazine* departs from its rapturous ravings about the fine fishing in Saratoga's North Platte River. (The same article shows a fisherman casting into Bird Cloud's deepest pool.) The author reported on a conversation between a visiting fisherman and two local men, one the owner of the hot springs.

> The forty-niners came through this part of the country and they brought a little smallpox along with 'em. That was new stuff for the Injuns and the first thing they knew, they had a fine hospital list, and they didn't know what was the matter.

24. Quoted in ibid., 192.

The medicine men went out and got orders to hike for Medicine Bow and the healing springs. They came in here by the hundreds with their sick and the medicine men built the tepees over the springs and herded the sick bucks into 'em and parboiled 'em for two or three days. Then one of the Comanche medicine men got a new message from the great spirit. The sick bucks weren't doing very well under the old treatment and this medicine man thought it would be a grand idea to take the patients out and heave 'em in the river and try cold water for a change. Nothing but running ice after around here in the spring, you know.

There were more good Indians around here that spring than ever before or since. Die? Say, they went bulging into the great hereafter ten abreast! First they were going to kill the medicine men, but then one of them got another wireless from the great spirit and sent out a signed statement that a curse had been put on the springs. Just the same as giving out word that the operation and treatment were highly successful, but the patient died. Since then the Injuns haven't come within forty miles of this place.[25]

The presence of the Indian past is strong at Bird Cloud because of the ancient campsites, arrowheads, stone knives, manos, rubbing stones and other tools that turn up, many made from material taken from the four chert quarries on the property. The evidence of people in the region long before the white explorers, army men, pioneers and ranchers came, especially along the river, is everywhere. My onetime neighbor, Ken Olson, found a bison skull, spear blades, arrowheads and much more from this

25. C. E. Van Loan, "The Greatest Trout-Fishing Town in the World," *Outing Magazine* 56, no. 4 (July 1910), 336–337.

and adjoining land over forty years. I too see Indian marks on the land and their lingering presence is never far away.

We were aware of archaeological possibilities from the first. While leveling the house site the James Gang discovered a deep fire pit full of charcoal under the area that became the dining room. We got back the report of an age of 2710 +/- 40 B.P. for the carbon 14 analysis, the Late Archaic period.

As we scraped and dug around the house area, fire pits emerged from under the tough grass, yielding chert flakes, an occasional hammerstone or a scraper, and one melted green glass bead no larger than a pinhead. The charcoal under the glass bead dated to 2410 +/- B.P., millennia before any trade beads came to North America and more than a thousand years before the sinewy Ancestral Puebloans (a.k.a. Anasazi) left their stronghold cliff dwellings. The archaeologist Dudley Gardner said insects or rodents might have carried the minuscule bead underground, or it may have been dropped by later people using an old fire ring. The fire ring area was barely an inch below the surface. This reassured me that there had been no great flood at the house site for more than two thousand years.

Most of the sites we found at Bird Cloud dated to the Late Archaic, 4600 to 2000 years B.P., and the stone grinding tools, the side-notched and corner-notched projectile points we turned up were characteristic of the period. The common foods of these people were large and small game animals either killed outright or scavenged, foraged plants, fruits, berries and winnowed seeds. The Archaic people also built semisubterranean pit houses with deep storage pits, hearth stones and reflector stones. During this period the climate was becoming drier, encouraging cacti and shrubs.

Bird Cloud and environs attracted Archaic period Indians because of the south-facing sites sheltered from the constant winds, the river and the creek that guaranteed game, the large numbers of nutritious wild plants, the good sight lines and defenses offered by the cliff, and the chert vein for toolmaking.

In this semiarid land water was the great wealth, then as now. The Indians used the North Platte River and Jack Creek not only to procure game, but for drinking, cooking, bathing, for thirsty horses (after the tribes of this region acquired them in the 1700s). Bison, deer, elk and pronghorn grazed the surrounding prairie. Mountain sheep lived in and along the cliff line. There were abundant jackrabbits and prairie dogs. Eagles and falcons nested in the crannied cliff, symbols of strength and sources of ceremonial feathers, and in the river lived waterfowl, beaver, muskrat and mink. Presumably there were fish—according to Seton-Karr only suckers until the state of Wyoming introduced rainbow trout in the late nineteenth century.[26] Today only the fish, raptors, deer, elk and pronghorn remain. Edible *Chenopodium,* Indian ricegrass, sego lily roots, yucca, biscuit-root, bloodroot and many other nutritious and medicinal plants still grow here.[27] The soil, though alkaline as short-grass soils are, has been enriched by centuries of river and creek silt deposition. Along the creek and the river shoreline grew willows and reeds likely used to make baskets and mats though we have found no evidence of these. In the cliff face, along a ridge half a mile back from it, and on a knoll near the east end are ancient chert quarries, the flake evidence of heavy use lying everywhere. Countless rounded river stones provided good hammers, and we sometimes found these tools, round and smooth

26. Seton-Karr, *My Sporting Holidays,* 268.

27. *Chenopodium* is a member of the goosefoot family. Huantzole, a vigorous spinachlike *Chenopodium,* is still grown in Mexico and in my garden. One May we were astounded to find a large draw on the top of the property crammed with thousands of sego lilies whose starchy tubers were prized by the Indians.

on the handhold end, abraded on the striking end. A few miles away the hot springs cured aches and illnesses. From the top of the cliff there were long views in every direction.

The cliff itself not only was a superb lookout point but may have been used as a bison or mountain sheep jump where hunters set up a drive line on the top and gradually forced the animals over the edge to their deaths below. Dave Quitter, the geologist and techie member of the James Gang, used Google Earth imaging to see if anything was visible from aloft. Satellite views showed a possible drive line of widely spaced stone clusters with a classic hook on one side near the brink. So much soil had covered these stones over the centuries and so many badgers, marmots, foxes, coyotes and prairie dogs had built and dug around them that they were almost impossible to see except in the satellite photo.

Dudley Gardner came to help us explore the base and face of the cliff where we surmised a bison drive *might* have ended and where we had seen a shallow cave that seemed blocked by carefully placed stones. We scratched around but did not find any bison remains in the colluvium pile below, and the seemingly carefully placed stones at the front of the shallow cave were only natural rockfall from the ceiling. But Deryl had spied a dark round spot high and to the left of the shallow cave the week before. We brought an old ladder along on this trip to get up to the spot and see what it was. I think we were all expecting something from the Indian past, but it turned out to be a 1917 penny. Someone had scraped out a penny-size circle in the rock and forced the coin in. It was badly corroded but had stayed in place for ninety years.

Higher up we could make out large letters scratched in the soft rock—J O H N S O N. Probably not Indian. I had seen a photograph taken in the 1880s showing Henry Seton-Karr's ranch-hands.[28] One of them, a boy in his teens sitting on the ground, was identified as Johnson. I surmised he might still have been working in the area in 1917, a tall, tough and lithe fellow in his forties by then and quite capable of climbing around on the cliff face and carving his name there. There was another inscription higher up and in an unknown language, very difficult to see. I wondered if it were Finnish, as there had been Finn settlers thirty miles northeast in the mining towns of Carbon and Hanna, and Dudley wondered if it were Mormon-related. And so high up that we could not reach it we could see another cave of fair size with something that looked like a large bone sticking out. Gerald vowed he would go down from the top on ropes and extract the bone. Perhaps it was a human bone, the site of an Indian burial. But that exploration would have to happen later.

Dudley returned weeks later and Gerald announced that the moment to pull the mystery bone out of the high cave was at hand. We all went across the river to the cliff, Dudley and I climbing down to the base, the James Gang on top with ropes and harness. Gerald came over the edge, lower and lower until he was at the mouth of the cave. I stood below, mouth agape, expecting we would see human remains. He grasped the bone and tugged. It was cemented into a pack rat midden with years of detritus and excrement. Gerald tried not to breathe in the effluvium and finally, with a mighty yank, he pulled the bone out. It was a short piece of what looked like a cow's leg. There was nothing else but the pack rat's personal effects.

There were scattered fire pits on the lower section of Bird Cloud, and on top. We found the chert vein by accident. I noticed chunks and flakes of chert near the cushion plant area at the west end of the cliff. The James Gang and I began explor-

28. See chapter 8 for Seton-Karr.

ing the west talus slope where a barely discernible trail angled down the steep, crumbly slope. Here the cliff was a series of shelves separated by steep colluvium deposits. It was possible to walk along the shelves. After an hour or so of exclaiming over the thousands of flakes of chert that littered the ground, we discovered a shoulder-height vein of glistening dark chert and followed it along for a quarter of a mile until the ledge we were walking on pinched out. Underfoot everywhere were thousands of flakes and larger fractured chunks, discarded small cutting tools and hammerstones.[29] Dudley called this a "lithic procurement site."

We traced the vein. The cliff bent to the northeast and on top the vein appeared again, running diagonally across the chalky two-track before disappearing into the sedge and sagebrush. It reappeared along a ridge half a mile distant, on a hogback near the north boundary. That vein was not as pronounced, nor the workings as obvious. It was also the lair of an exceptionally large rattlesnake which pleased Dudley, a thwarted herpetologist, and showed once again on the flanks of an eroding knoll. Dudley remarked later in a report that the chert materials "represent the entire lithic reduction sequence core, primary, secondary, tertiary, and micro flakes."[30] He also, after our many walks over the property, noted five types of sites in addition to the quarries. They were open campsites, lithic scatters, rock art, historic sites and isolated artifacts.

The James Gang and I became intensely interested in the traces of the bygone time when the Indians were on the land. Dudley generously agreed to excavate in the rare times when

29. Flakes are the tiny chips of stone that are broken off the piece of chert someone is trying to make into a projectile point. This is not a lost art. There are many flint knappers today who can make beautiful points and tools.
30. Dudley Gardner, *Report 3* (December 30, 2009), 2.

he was in the area and had a few hours or days free. He showed us how to look and what to look for. We became alert to fire-cracked rocks on the surface, arrowheads, stones that showed signs of use.

He said we could do a practice dig at the east end of the property in a sandy area at a site with fire-cracked rocks—a site already disturbed by a badger. We painstakingly measured out the plot, divided it into squares with stakes and string and began to scrape and dig. The soil went into buckets and the buckets were emptied onto a meshed sorting screen which caught many, many chert flakes. The wind rose and threw dirt and sand at us, despite Gerald's quick plywood windbreak. In addition to the flakes we uncovered two dozen fire-scorched rocks, a biface (knife), a broken piece of fossiliferous chert that had been heated. Dudley said a cow had stepped on it.

In the years after I bought the Bird Cloud property Dudley narrowed the sites worth exploration down to three: the Under Penny site, the Falling Cow site and a series of sand dunes at the back of the top plateau. The sand dunes showed little after a shovel test, but the Under Penny, which was an assemblage of fire-cracked rock and some charcoal, yielded an age of 1030 +/- B.P. and indications of *Chenopodium* and mountain sheep remains.

Eventually Dudley looked at and mapped the Falling Cow site, and agreed that it was worth a bit of digging. The site was a gradually sloping ridge with a south face nearer the river and a north face a few hundred feet distant. We saw a pink quartz arrowhead and a scraper on one strew of fire-cracked rock. The lithic debris was primarily moss agate, a cream-colored chert and the root-beer-colored chert from the four quarries on the property. We could see several more fire pits in an area of a few acres. A deep gulley ran down to the river.

Dudley's visits were very widely spaced and the digging sporadic, but in 2009 he came with Martin Lammers, a historian turned archaeologist, and several students. They started excavating three fire pits on the south side of the ridge where the soil was a thin, eolian deposit overlying regolith, or crumbled rough rock. The flora was sagebrush and sedges and some grass. Martin said the wiry black roots of the sedge were almost impossible to cut through. It became quite clear that more than five hundred acres of sedge at the top of the cliff were holding the soil in place in defiance of the hurricane-force winds that tore over them. These profuse, tangled roots as fine as thread and as strong as steel form an almost impenetrable mat just below the soil surface.

Those first south-side pits yielded some charcoal, broken rocks and a few flakes and chips where some ancient hunter had worked or reworked his stone tools. The radiocarbon assay of charcoal from one of these fire pits gave an age of 1580 +/- 40 B.P. Deryl noticed two other fire pit areas a few hundred feet farther back from the river on the north slope of the ridge. Here the soil was deeper and there were some old sand dunes. Dudley began to dig one of the north side pits.

In September 2009 Dudley was working on the site, and the James Gang and I met him there one late afternoon. The lowering sun cast a rich shadow-throwing light over the area and we could see objects that had been invisible in stronger light. In the lee of a sage bush I found a tiny agate (or chert) knife the size of my thumbnail, the serrated edge still wickedly sharp. Then Gerald found one. And another. Agate has a cool, almost slippery feel, very pleasurable to the hand. We soon had a dozen little knives, all of white agate, and it seemed we might have stumbled on either the site of a skinning party or a tool shop as some of the edges were dull and some very sharp and showing slanted abrasion marks on the cutting edges. Would we find bones or toolmaking flakes?

And where did the agate originate? Dudley thought it might have come from the nearby knoll quarry so we climbed up and looked for a match. The chert here was mostly root beer color, definitely not the source of our small knives. The agate might also have been carried from the cliff or the rattlesnake quarry. Careful examination and geochemical analysis could probably match the tools with their quarry source, a task for the future.

It was on the way back from the knoll to the dig site that I found a beautiful chunk of glassy black obsidian, highly prized for projectile points and not known at Bird Cloud or any nearby place. Dudley said the most likely source of this chunk was the famous Obsidian Cliff in Yellowstone, a mother source of prehistoric artifacts. Yellowstone obsidian objects have been found in Canada, Washington, Idaho, Wyoming, Montana, Michigan, Ohio, Illinois, Iowa, Kansas, South Dakota and North Dakota. Someone had carried it more than three hundred miles from Yellowstone to Bird Cloud.

The fire pit Dudley worked on now was different. In addition to the usual soot-stained stones he found a flat rock set on end, probably a heat deflector. This made him think he might be exhuming a pit house. The entire area began to grow in our minds as a possible cluster of pit houses where people stayed for varying periods. Later Dudley wrote:

The current theory about potential structures like the one at Falling Cow is to not so much look at them as pit houses but as structures set into sand that took on a basin shape out of use and via construction methods. For argument purposes let's assume the structure was a dome shaped hide structure. The frame for the dome could be either from sage, willow, pine, or even woven grasses. The builders scooped out the sand and leveled the floor, then set the frame on the leveled sand. The hide was then placed on the [frame] and more sand was placed on the edges of the hide to keep out the wind. Inside the small domed structure . . . sat or lay the occupants. Normal use caused the sand to dish out. . . . If a central hearth was set inside the structure the center would be lower or higher based on preference—but here fire cracked rock would be evident—either because they were used as boiling stones or some other heating function. Over time a very distinct feature would appear but since these were often only short term occupation structures a well defined interior feature system might not have been employed (e.g., storage pits, etc.).[31]

Dudley's digging did not show the typical concave shape for a house pit. The most he would say is that he felt people "created a depression in the sand and set a superstructure over the small depression. We need more data to confirm this hypothesis but we do feel we have some evidence of a habitation in the dunes."[32]

The idea of this site as a short-term shelter camp seemed likely. On the south side of the ridge there was evidence of six or eight campfires spread over several acres. We all walked many times through the sagebrush in the area, peering at the ground, looking for further signs of occupation. I found a mano, a river rock with one side worn silky smooth from grinding, near one of the cracked rock circles. With a mano and a flat stone or hollowed rock one could grind wild grains and

31. Ibid. It should be noted that Archaic pit houses in Wyoming were older than and vastly different from the deep and elaborate pit houses with storage pits, vent holes and partitions in the southwest, as at Mesa Verde.
32. Unpublished letter to Annie Proulx.

seeds into nutritious flour. I did not find a flat stone that might have served as a metate. Next year . . .

Walking on the land or digging in the fine soil I am intensely aware that time quivers slightly, changes occurring in imperceptible and minute ways, accumulating so subtly that they seem not to exist. Yet the tiny shifts in everything—cell replication, the rain of dust motes, lengthening hair, wind-pushed rocks—press inexorably on and on.

CHAPTER 10

A Year of Birds

prairie falcon
high-speed flier
– the terror of the cliff –

Pelecanus erythrorhynchos
fabulous flier, arrived at
Bird Cloud April 14, 2010 – earlier than usual

The first day I saw Bird Cloud, in July 2003, I was astonished by the great number and variety of birds in this river habitat. A bald eagle sat in a tree near the river's edge. Pelicans sailed downstream. I saw swallows, falcons, bluebirds. Flocks of ducks burst up from the North Platte and flew over my head in whistling flight. Ravens croaked from the cliff. I thought my great avocation for the rest of my life would be watching these birds and learning their ways. I decided to keep a notebook of bird behaviors and daily routines. I planned to buy a telescope when I could afford it and put it upstairs, aimed at the river

191

and the cliff. Harry Teague had included a narrow tall window in the library that framed the eagles' favorite perch tree, an old cottonwood snag. But the tree fell down in a windstorm as the James Gang was finishing the house, and the eagles shifted to another tree, neither quite so choice, nor aligned with the special window.

Through the two-year building of the house I had tried to identify the habits of the birds in the area, and gradually recognized seasonal waves of avian inhabitants. Watching a large number of birds took concentration and time—there was nothing casual about it. The bald eagles were permanent residents. Some hawks stayed and some hawks went south. The great horned owls stayed. The ravens raised a family every year and then went somewhere else to hunt once the young began flying. They came back in autumn to tidy up the nest and poke around, then departed again before the winter storms came. But I saw ravens constantly throughout the winter, mostly at higher elevations or along roadsides feeding on vehicle-killed carcasses, so perhaps the highway carnage was beneficial to the meat-eating birds. The roadkill ravens had developed a good sense of timing, staying on the carcass as cars approached, and flying up at the last moment. Only rarely did a fan of black feathers near the remains of a squashed rabbit show that one bird had lost the game of chicken and itself become food. Meadowlarks came in early spring to eat the seeds of a particular weed that grew to the south of the house, and after a few weeks they were gone.

Migration for some birds, maybe all, does not seem to be a do-or-die, single-destination journey, but a more leisurely series of shorter flights with stops at known places with good comestibles. I noticed with consternation that after Deryl and Dave made a beautiful (to human eyes) garden where the favored weeds once grew, the meadowlarks went somewhere else. But what were those weeds we replaced with needle-and-thread grasses that bent in the wind, flashing glassy stems as fine as pen strokes? None of us can remember. In early spring hundreds of red-winged blackbirds hit the copper-stemmed willows on the island and the cliff echoed their yodeling *"aujourd'hui! aujourd'hui!"* A northern flicker, outraged at the sight of the house going up, hammered violently on it to warn the James Gang that this was his habitat, his territory, take this damn house apart and *git!* A photographer friend, Marty Stupich, had taken pictures of the cliff from an airplane and enlarged them in a five-foot-long photograph on which I could mark the nests of cliff-dwelling birds. Because the altitude of the plane showed a different cliff face angle than I saw when standing on the ground, many of the crannies and ledges favored by birds did not show well. An artist friend made a detailed drawing based on the photograph and the view from the ground, giving me a somewhat better map of the choicest aeries and declivities. I put out feeders to attract the smaller birds, but days, weeks and months went by with no avian visitors. These wild birds were too naïve to recognize feeders as a source of food.

On December 30, 2006, after three years of anxiety, bill paying, construction and shuttling back and forth through the Medicine Bows, I was suddenly alone for the first time at Bird Cloud. I was impressed that during the two years of construction the bald eagles stuck around. The relevant Stokes handbook stated: "Once a pair is established on a territory, they are very reluctant to move elsewhere to breed."[1] That fit the case. Stokes also warned readers from the "egg-laying to early nest-

<hr />

1. *Stokes Field Guide to Birds: Western Region* 3 (New York: Little, Brown, 1996), 83–84.

ing" period to stay at least a quarter of a mile away from the nest as alarmed parents might abandon their nest or the young. But these eagles hadn't read Stokes and tolerated all of us. The house itself was roughly a quarter of a mile from the nest and the eagles only warned us away if we stood on the riverbank directly across from the nest or got over to the other side of the water and walked near their tree. Then, in 2008 they built a new nest directly above the river and closer to our house. Since then the bald eagles have raised two chicks every year except one year when only a single chick survived. The books say one surviving chick is the norm, but these eagles have been calm and laid-back—wonderful parents with a high success rate. Whenever strangers came to the house the bald eagles took turns flying over and scrutinizing them. Anything new—lawn chair, garden hose, shrubs—piqued their curiosity and they flew over, low and slow, examining the object. In fact, they were nosy. It was quite fair. I peered at them through binoculars, they peered back.

On that red-letter day when I was alone in the house for the first time one eagle sat in a favorite perch tree across the river. The day before both of them sat side by side for hours, gazing down through the pale water sliding over the rocks, waiting for incautious fish. This was eagle-style fishing. Sometimes they stood in the shallows, cold water soaking their fancy leggings. Bald eagles are skillful at their trade and we have seen them haul fish out of the freezing water onto the ice, or swoop down, sink their talons into a big trout and rise up with the heavy fish twisting futilely. The James Gang was lucky enough to see one of them dive onto a large fish, lock its talons, then struggle to get into the air with the heavy load, meanwhile riding the fish like a surfboard down the rushing river.

Walking induces a trancelike state that allows the mind freedom and ease and encourages exploration of odd possibilities and improbable connections. I walked every day, for the mind as well as the body. On that first solitary day at Bird Cloud, I walked east to the Jack Creek bridge and looked up at a big empty nest high on the cliff across the river. It was clearly an eagle nest. Had the bald eagles used it before moving half a mile west to the cottonwoods? Had it belonged to another pair of eagles? The huge structure was heaped with snow. Somehow it had a fierce look, black and bristling with stick ends. At 4:30 sunlight still plated the cliff with gold light. Ten minutes later it had faded to cardboard grey. I looked again at the distant nest, then noticed that on the debris pile of colluvium below and a little to the west of the nest there were two elk. They were likely refugees from a big herd that had moved through the property several weeks earlier. Twenty or thirty geese flew upriver high enough to be out of gun range. Dusk thickened, and then, in the gloaming, I saw a large bird fly into a cranny directly above the elk. Roosting time for someone, but who?

The next day—the last day of a miserable year—the sun cleared the Medicine Bows at 7:45. It was a beautiful, clear winter morning, the sun sparkling on the snow, no wind, two degrees below zero and a setting moon that was almost full. As Richard Lassels, a seventeenth-century guide for the Grand Tour said of fireflies, "Huge pretty, methought."[2] By noon both bald eagles were in the trees above the river about five hundred feet apart, watching for fish below. After half an hour they flew upriver to try their luck in another stretch of water.

In midmorning out of the corner of my eye I saw a large bird flying upriver with steady, brisk flaps and remembered the large bird I had seen the previous evening taking shelter in

2. Geoffrey Trease, *The Grand Tour: A History of the Golden Age of Travel* (New York: Holt, Rinehart and Winston, 1967), 2.

a cranny near the big empty nest. Was it the same bird? What was it? It was too big to be a hawk. It wasn't a bald eagle; their brilliant white heads and tails make them unmistakable. Hoping for another glimpse of the big bird I skied down to the east end of the property, a cottonwood bosque that the river floods in spring and where thousands of young willows sprout anew each year. Skiing was unpleasant as vast numbers of snowshoe hares had gnawed the willows down to projecting stubs and stamped the snow into a lumpy floor. This was the Big Rabbit Restaurant. A downy woodpecker pounded on the old dead cottonwood that resembled a David Nash sculpture.

The days were too short for complete happiness and the dregs of sunlight dripped off the cliff at 4:42. A few moments later I just missed seeing the mysterious big bird, caught only a fractional look as it sailed into the same cranny as yesterday.

New Year's Day was warm and sunny, 32°F, encouraging a few foolish blades of grass to emerge from the snow. A flock of goldeneyes, diving underwater to forage, dominated a section of the river that stayed open all winter. I thought there might be a hot spring in that part of the river that kept it clear of ice. This was winter range for these hardy ducks which breed and summer in Canada.

At the end of the daylight the bald eagles sat in trees three hundred yards apart, merging into the dusk but still staring into the river. Their low-light vision must be good. At 4:40 a dozen Canada geese flew upstream. An orange ribbon lay on the western horizon. I waited, binoculars in hand. Two minutes later the last sunlight licked the top of the cliff, then was gone. The sky turned purple to display a moon high and full. I did not see the large mystery bird. Perhaps it was an owl and had no problem flying after dark. But I doubted it. I had a strong suspicion that it was an eagle, the owner of the big sinister nest.

All the next day I unpacked books, too busy to watch birds. The James Gang came and so did the men with the granite counters for the kitchen. A day or so later the thermometer zoomed up to 40°F, but a rude breeze sucked any transient warmth away. The bald eagles took their stations above the river, waiting for careless fish to show themselves. I ran errands in town and on the way back in late afternoon saw a great blue heron flying toward the river. What was it doing in Wyoming at the coldest time of year? At the front gate I was surprised to see a woman with a camera. She said she was Mary Magdalena, an artist, and would use her sunset photos to later work into paintings. My mother had been a painter, too, but always spurned working from photographs as somehow ignoble.

The warm day immediately became only a memory. Back to zero temps. The river pinched in, making waists of black water in the ice. I saw no goldeneyes and thought they might have retreated to a warmer section of river. I skied near the west corner, not noticing the bald eagle in the boundary tree. I got too close and it flapped away. Remorsefully I skied east. There was a hole in my glove and one hand got very cold. The sky colors were exquisite pastels, the Medicine Bows misty with distant falling snow.

For me the keeping of a list of birds sighted has neither value nor interest. I'm not that kind of bird-watcher, though I do watch them with pleasure and do try to identify species new to me. But I am more interested in birds of particular places, how they behave over longer periods of time and how they use their chosen habitats—a more holistic view than a list of "I-saw-them." At Bird Cloud some birds were year-round residents while most were summer visitors. Eagles, northern harriers, goldeneyes and woodpeckers stuck out the winters while the prairie and peregrine falcons, swallows, bluebirds, and a hundred others brought and took the changing seasons with them. What the birds did, ate, raised attracted me. I suppose I could say I was drawn to their stories. But in thinking about all this the next morning I once again missed seeing the big mystery bird. In the fleeting seconds it was in view I saw it was completely dark in color. The rhythm of its wing beats was similar to that of an eagle. Could it be a juvenile bald eagle from last year's hatch? Or was it a golden? Maybe. The wind came up and harsh, blowing snow and cold moved in.

Then came days of flailing west wind, strong enough to push its snout under the crust of the fallen snow wherever the hares or I had left footprints, strong enough to then flip up big pancakes of crust and send them cartwheeling east until they disintegrated in puffs of snow. Eagles love strong wind. It is impossible to miss the joy they take in exhibition flying. The bald pair were out playing in the fierce gusts, mounting higher and higher until they were specks, then splitting apart and going upriver and downstream. After a few minutes of empty sky the unknown big dark bird flapped briefly into view before disappearing in a snow squall. Surely it couldn't be a turkey vulture at this time of year! Could it? I was missing something obvious.

Late in the afternoon as dusk crept up the eastern rim of the world one of the bald eagles showed up with talons full of branches and dropped out of sight at the nest tree. Were they redecorating the nest on a bitterly cold, windy winter day? The wind swelled and blustered. A solitary duck appeared, blown all over the place. White underside and black head and wings and was that a round white spot on its face?—probably a goldeneye but for a second it resembled a penguin shot out of a cannon. Half an hour later two more east-bound ducks appeared clocking along with the wind at about eighty miles an hour. The second bald eagle came into sight fighting the head-wind, just hanging in the air and flapping vainly, until finally it turned and in seconds was miles away. The nest eagle rose up and followed.

The next morning the wind had calmed to thirty miles an hour with gusts hitting fifty. It was a cold and sunny day and the bald eagle team was out flying at eight. As I made coffee I saw the big mystery bird just flapping out of sight toward the TA Ranch. Why was it so elusive? I wanted badly to get a good look at it, but it seemed to fly past only when my head was turned. The two isolated elk stood on a knoll at the west end of the cliff; antlerless, dark brown necks, yellow rumps and red-brown body color. At first sight I could imagine they were the mountain sheep that used to live on the cliff in Indian times. Their faces seemed rather dished, like sheep faces. Magpies were busy across the river, and one raven sat in a tree slightly to the west of their nest site in the cliff. Could the raven, like the eagle, be interested in fixing up its nest so early in the year?

By afternoon the wind was up again and at the top of the sky were three eagle-shaped specks, whirling and wheeling. Three eagles playing in the wind. Three? Was one of them a juvenile bald planning to nest here, or was it the big mystery bird? And just how many eagles called this cliff home?

That night the wind went berserk, terrific shrieking and battering. In the morning it was still intense and I could see the big windows moving slightly in and out. The worst wind yet. I went out into the driveway to see how badly it was drifted. Huge impassable drifts. The wind almost knocked me over. A small bird shot past the kitchen window, but on the far side of the river the two bald eagles sat calmly in the trees near their nest. How could they stand it?

During the nights of high-velocity wind I lay tense and

awake in the dark listening to the bellowing and roar as it tried to blow the house over. In daytime, working and unpacking books, it was easier to ignore it. The television sets would not work because the wind had wrenched the dish out of alignment. After four or five days of relentless howling the wind fell into a temporary coma, turning everything over to a warm, sunny and calm day. Temperatures climbed into the forties. But the weather report warned another storm was approaching. The James Gang smashed a narrow alley through the drifts on the county road and cleared out the driveway. I was no longer snowbound. The power company made it out and realigned the satellite dish.

The sunlight hours were lengthening by a few minutes each day. While it was calm I walked down to the east end of the property, and glancing up at the cliff I saw not one, but two big dark birds. They were playing in the air, obviously delighted with the calm air, with each other, with life in general. Then they both dove into their bedroom niche in the chimney west of the big empty nest. While they were flying I could not hear their voices because a large flock of ducks, more than a hundred, flew over, twittering and whistling. The big dark birds looked like eagles, they flew like eagles, but they were completely dark. They did not have the golden napes pictured in the bird books. I told myself I had to watch carefully from now on. Goldens soar with a slight dihedral; bald eagles soar with their wings almost flat. But I was now almost sure that a pair of golden eagles owned the big nest and were preparing to use it.

The next day started out warm, calm and sunny but another three-day storm was on the way and by late morning low, malignant clouds smothered the ranges in all directions. The weather people said it was going to turn very cold. I took advantage of the lull before the storm to get outdoors with the binoculars. A raven was fooling around the cliff face, trying out several niches. Then the big dark birds appeared above the cliff in a tumbling display. The binoculars showed that they did have lighter necks and heads. I had no doubt now. They were a pair of golden eagles and they were courting, planning to fix up the big empty nest and raise a family only half a mile from the bald eagles. I felt fabulously wealthy with a bald eagle nest and a golden eagle nest both visible from my dining room window. I wanted to spend the day watching them, but the storm was due to hit during the night so I headed out to get groceries and supplies while the road was still open.

January wore on. The bald eagles were up early and used the mornings for fishing, sitting immobile side by side in the dead tree at the river's edge. It was cold and day after day the snow fell as in Conrad Aiken's story "Silent Snow, Secret Snow" which I read when I was eight years old, thinking it was a story about a profound snowfall. Later, when I learned it was an oblique study of intensifying juvenile madness I was disappointed. On the frozen river four coyotes nosed around the north shore margins. Upstream the goldeneyes' strip of water was still open but daily shrinking.

On a Sunday morning of flat calm it was 21°F below zero. The air was stiff. Freezing river mist had coated every tree and shrub. There were no birds in sight. The sun struggled up and the mist rose in great humps over the remaining ribbons of open water. The tops of the cottonwoods glittered like icy nosegays, stems wrapped in gauze. Spring seemed very far away, but the bald eagle pair sat side by side catching the first rays. They often sat this way, side by side, one great eagle-beast with two heads. Was it for warmth? Was it to renew their bond? Were they like an old married couple who have become companions? Or was it hormonal stirrings? Whatever, it was a fine thing to see. As the sun gained height the eagles fluffed themselves out and began to preen. A lone magpie flew over the mist. In the afternoon I skied down to the east end and into the cottonwood bosque to a corner I once thought would be a good place to put up a tent. There was one golden eagle and four magpies eating the scanty remains of a snowshoe hare. The eagle fled as I came in sight, the magpies went reluctantly, sure I was after their feast. It was easy to see what had happened. The hare's tracks zigged and zagged through the brush, but twelve inches east of the corpse I saw the snow-angel wing prints of the attacking eagle.

On the summer day the James Gang and I found the chert vein in the west end of the cliff we came upon a curious puzzle. On one ledge with a sheltering overhang there were hundreds of dry sticks scattered around, and more in an intertwined tangle that seemed to be the base of a gigantic nest. We decided it was an old eagle nest that something had destroyed. Looking around we spotted a ten-foot length of rusted heavy wire, one end wrapped securely around a twenty-pound rock. We couldn't get past the idea that the free end of the wire had once been attached to some kind of trap, that someone had wanted a live eagle. It was not hard to imagine the eagle ripping its own nest apart in a savage effort to get free. There is not a way to know what happened.

Wyoming was once a haven for eagle killers. In the bad old days in this valley in the 1960s and '70s many men who are now cattlemen raised sheep and firmly believed that bald and golden eagles carried off young lambs. If you raised sheep you killed eagles—bald or golden, but especially golden eagles, though both birds were protected by law. Poison (thallium sulfate was a favorite), or shotgun from rented helicopters and small planes, or sharpshooters from open pickup windows were the preferred modi operandi. Eagle populations declined. Gerald remembers one eagle killer near Saratoga who came around to brag about his kills. Eagles were killed in other states, especially in the west, but Wyoming became notorious to the U.S. Fish and Wildlife Service, the Audubon Society, and to newspaper readers across the country as the home ground of the most ignorant, blatant and vicious eagle-killing ranchers. Chief among them was the wealthy and powerful sheep rancher, Herman Werner, ex-president of the Wyoming Stock Growers Association, one of "The Wyoming Helicopter Monsters," as Michael Frome, the distinguished environmental journalist, labeled them, from the Casper and Buffalo area, using a hired helicopter based in Buffalo to "sluice" eagles.[3] Werner had ranches near Casper and Saratoga. Nathaniel Reed, the assistant secretary of the interior under Richard Nixon, made stopping the killings a primary goal.

In 1971 the FBI set up an eagle sting. An agent who was raised in the west posed as a ranchhand and got a job on Werner's spread where, in the bunkhouse, he heard about dozens of dead eagles. Because this was hearsay, a federal judge would not issue a search warrant. But Bart Rea, an Audubon member who had been monitoring the eagle killings, and his friend, another Audubon member, were out at the airfield one day and both men happened to notice someone working on a nearby helicopter. They could see a shotgun and empty shells in the craft. The friend had his camera with him and used it. The man working on the helicopter realized he had been photographed. Weeks later the anxiety-ridden helicopter pilot showed up at the Department of the Interior in Washington. He said

3. Michael Frome cited in Dennis Drabelle, "Unfair Game," *Audubon,* January–February 2008, 5; "Environment: Sluicing the Eagles," *Time,* August 16, 1971.

that if he were granted immunity he'd tell about the eagle killings, and so he did, testifying to a Senate subcommittee that he had carried eagle-hunting shooters into the Wyoming skies, that Werner was one of the air service's best customers, and that the gunners had shot more than five hundred bald and golden eagles. *Time* magazine reported the Wyoming dead eagle count was 770.[4] Despite "national outrage" the department was still not able to get a search warrant for Werner's land. But the U.S. Air Force, testing new surveillance planes, flew over the ranch and an infrared camera lit up a pile of decomposing flesh. That finally got the search warrant and the discovery of eagle carcasses in number.

> There was still a hitch. The U.S. attorney for Wyoming balked at bringing a case against the rancher because he was sure that Herman Werner would never be convicted by a Wyoming jury. Werner . . . made a surprise visit to [Nathaniel] Reed's office. "He simply bolted in," Reed remembers, "a wiry man wearing a Stetson hat. He said he was going to get me. I said quietly, 'Before you get me, please tell me who you are.' He said 'I am Herman Werner, the man who protects his sheep by killing eagles. And you don't know anything about eagles.'"[5]

The tough alternative newspaper, *High Country News,* took up the cause and Wyoming public opinion began to quiver and shift. The U.S. attorney general pressed for prosecution. But Werner never came to trial. A few months before the trial was to begin he was killed in a car wreck. In Wyoming, as the wool market declined and sheepmen turned to cattle, as the fine for

4. Ibid.
5. Drabelle, "Unfair Game."

killing eagles greatly increased, as ranchers began to learn that the Department of the Interior had sharp teeth and that bald eagles were interested in carrion and fish, not lambs, the killings virtually stopped.

Two very Wyoming touches to the whole affair are the commemorative Herman Werner Reservoir Number 1 in Converse County, and the Werner Wildlife Museum at Casper College. The museum includes "an extensive bird collection." Wyoming irony.

The helicopter shootings got national coverage, but eagle electrocution stories stay in the ecological and wildlife magazines. In 2009 PacifiCorp, a monster electric utility spread over the west, was fined $10.5 million for killing eagles and other birds in Wyoming by electrocution. Between January 2007 and July 2009, PacifiCorp fried 232 Wyoming eagles with its old transmission equipment. It is on probation and has been ordered to retrofit the equipment. It can't happen quickly enough.

Every morning in January 2007 there were a dozen jackrabbits and cottontails around the house, digging through the snow for frozen grass. When we drove down the entrance road there were always two or three dodging and leaping in front of the truck. Finally, after weeks of swinging in the wind, the bird feeder attracted a clientele—around fifty grey-crowned rosy-finches. A magpie in a tree on the island wondered what the fuss was all about. For rosy-finches the flock is everything. It is a unit with many small parts held together by some kind of group consciousness in flight and feeding. In a flock there is less exposure to predators—the "selfish herd" effect? Stokes said that birds tend to bunch together in fall and winter and that there is a hierarchy within the flock. So far any hierarchy eluded me.

Colorado was hit with its fifth big snowstorm in five weeks.

At Bird Cloud snow and cold alternated, and there was a very heavy rime frost on the willows and trees along the river. The finch flock grew ever larger with rosies apparently coming in from everywhere. Chris Fisher in *Birds of the Rocky Mountains* put it well: "During the winter, Gray-crowned Rosy Finches spill out of the attics of the Rockies to flock together at lower elevations."[6] So they were likely coming into this valley from both the Sierra Madre and the Medicine Bow. At and around the feeder there were eighty to ninety finches. They rose into the sky for no reason I could ascertain, wheeled about and returned to the feeder. There were no birds of prey in sight, no humans, no dogs or cows or snares, the wind was calm and the day sunny. Did they all fly up to gain elevation and spy out the land for distant threats? Or to reassert the (to me, invisible) hierarchy? Sometimes they flew to the trees near the river for a few minutes, then back to the feeder. I had to refill the thing several times a day.

Days later the magpie that had watched the mob of finches for a week, now ventured to approach the cafeteria and found a few seeds on the ground. How long, I wondered, before he or she brought in friends and relatives? The magpie concentrated on the big rock beneath the feeder which likely had tasty seeds lodged in its crevices as I often hurled handfuls of seeds over a wide area. The finches continued to help themselves at the feeder. The magpie eyed them. The magpie hopped to the top of the wire fence around the feeder tree and gazed at the feeder. All the finches flew up suddenly and the magpie leapt into space. The finches circled back sans magpie. It was time to make another trip to the feed store for more seed.

6. Chris C. Fisher, *Birds of the Rocky Mountains* (Edmonton, A. B., and Renton, Wash.: Lone Pine Publishing, 1997), 298.

The beautiful days had grown longer. In the morning I watched one of the bald eagles dive toward an open stretch of water off the island and I ran madly upstairs with the binoculars just in time to see it heave a fish onto the ice. It ate part of the fish then flew to the nest. At ten minutes past five the sun still gilded the top fifty feet of the cliff. One bald eagle was in the nest tree, the other flying downriver. The cliff turned the color of a russet apple and I enjoyed the rare deep orange sunset smoldering under the edge of a dark dirty-sock cloud.

The highways were miraculously clear and dry in early February 2007 and I went to Santa Fe for a week to let the James Gang finish up some work in the house. Global warming got to Bird Cloud before I came back and for the first time in months the ground was visible. The road in and our lane were quagmires of heavy mud. The county actually ran a snowplow up to our gate for the first and last time. The cliff was still sunlit at 5:30 and the two elk were still hanging around the cliff. The rosy-finches smothered the feeder as soon as I refilled it with fresh groceries. Several magpies watched from the island. On my first morning back only one eagle sat in the fishing tree. The other was on the nest and I supposed he/she was sitting on eggs. A real sign of spring. I stayed far away from the goldens' nest as they were skittish and shy and I did not want them to abandon it. I thought bald eagles must lay and hatch their eggs earlier than the goldens. I knew I should look this up, but did not.

In order not to disturb the goldens I gave up skiing to the east end of the property and went instead to the Sierra Madre trails. I stopped for gas at the Encampment Trading Post one morning and a Forest Service truck pulled up for some of the same. The driver said he had just finished grooming the ski trails (something that almost never happened on the east slope when I lived in Centennial). The trails were beautiful and the skiing perfect despite heavy snow showers which I like. On the way home I saw a golden eagle dining on a roadside deer carcass. Was it one of the Bird Cloud goldens?

On my way back from Santa Fe I had bought a telescope and set it up in my bedroom which has a grand view of the river and the cliff. The eagles weren't in sight but one of the elk was. Oddly, it seemed to be wearing a canvas jacket, different and lighter in color than the neck and haunches. Was it a trick of the light? It looked like a boulder in the middle. After an hour the elk stood up and disclosed the second elk lying close behind it. With the telescope details leapt into prominence. The first elk pulled some tufts of hair from its back, then nibbled on sage or rabbitbrush. The second elk became invisible again. There looked to be well over a hundred rosy-finches at the feeder. But where were the fine ravens who raised a crowd every year on a high ledge of the cliff directly across the river?

Ten days into February 2007 came one of those anomaly days, warm and cloudy. I woke to the spatter of rain. The forecast said it would turn to snow by afternoon. I wondered about the ravens. Shouldn't they at least be bringing twigs to the nest ledge? Ehrlich, Dobkin and Wheye said that the male, with some help from the female, builds the nest; that she lays four to six eggs; that they both sit on the eggs; that incubation is eighteen to twenty-one days and that the young fly after thirty-eight to forty-four days.[7] So, if they fly, as they have the past two years, around Memorial Day, then they must hatch around April 20–25, and the eggs must be laid the first week in April. They are monogamous birds. Late in the afternoon, as if it had

7. Paul R. Ehrlich, David S. Dobkin, and Darryl Wheye, *The Birder's Handbook: A Field Guide to the Natural History of North American Birds* (New York: Simon & Schuster, 1988), 420.

read my thoughts, one raven appeared, sailing around the cliff, legs hanging down as though prepared to land. It flew into the deep chimney to the west of the old nest site several times. That would be a better place to nest if the ravens wanted more privacy and shelter from the southwest winds, but for me the view would not be good. The elk were still around.

Ehrlich et al. also wrote that rosy-finches build nests in cliffs and crevices in alpine tundra and maritime islands. They too are monogamous. The finches at the feeder were just winter visitors, not residents, but they could be breeding in the Medicine Bow or Sierra Madre. The two goldens sailed around their big nest all afternoon. One perched on the projecting rock at the top of the cliff. With the telescope I could see the golden hood rather well. In the vicinity of the raven nest a prairie falcon flashed into sight. I remembered seeing one in that area last summer. I had no idea what trouble that bird would cause the local residents. The bald eagle pair came flying down the river on their way home. The goldens seemed to chase them for a few hundred yards and then turned back to the big nest area and one flew back up to the projecting rock. When they came in for landings their wings looked very broad and bent into huge hoops. The balds were soaring high, maybe looking for food. What a show, and all from my dining room window.

Bird life was picking up as beetles and worms began to stir in the earth. Early the next morning a northern harrier sat on an electric pole but fortunately did not make the killing contact. I spent the day shelving more books and writing and at sunset, without thinking, I tried to walk along the river but the goldens became so agitated that I turned back. One golden angrily escorted me all the way to the house. I had once thought of inviting bird-watchers onto the property but I knew then that was impossible. The goldens had to have privacy.

A few days later I went for an evening walk on the old property line road, keeping a quarter-mile distance between myself and the goldens. They came out but they did not call, just flew along the cliff, watching me. Near the end of the property another pair of goldens appeared, silent and flying rather low as though also checking me out. Suddenly the nest pair came roaring east along the cliff and drove the strange pair away. I could see them settling in a tree to the east. Perhaps they were nesting there. Six eagles in three pairs in the space of a mile.

The next morning one of the bald eagles and the prairie falcon had a sky-filling quarrel, the falcon darting, the eagle wheeling and swooping. The falcon suddenly disappeared. At noon the wind began to rise and in an hour it was lashing the cottonwoods. One of the bald eagles sat on a branch above the river watching for fish. The branch moved to and fro vigorously. With each lurch the eagle braced its tail against the branch like a woodpecker, and for some reason I found this endearing. Sometimes I thought of these birds as Evan Connell's Mr. and Mrs. Bridge. The falcon flew around near the goldens' part of the cliff. The big birds were not in sight. Something about the falcon's busybody day bothered me. Was it looking for a nest site? In previous years they had nested at the far east end of the cliff near another pair of prairie falcons. Every bird a falcon came near seemed agitated.

Great blue-black clouds rolled in from the west and just at dusk I saw one raven slide into the lower level of the chimney. I was sure it was abandoning the old ledge nest site.

Sunny, warm, a little wind and the smell of spring. One of the balds waded in the river and caught something small. The goldens were on their high promontory. One hopped down eight or ten feet and seemed to be taking a dust bath, then it zoomed to the nest and sat on it for a few minutes. I noticed there were some new sticks protruding. In a few more minutes she (I am guessing) was back on the promontory. As the day ended the swollen buds of the cottonwoods seemed to have been sprayed with bronze. One of the balds drifted near the golden nest and was chased home for its trespass. A pair of Canada geese, the first this year, flew upstream. The sunlight went off the cliff at 5:33 and in its last flash I saw the elk in silhouette at the west end. The huge yellow colossus of crumbling stone held the light as the sky darkened. How many thousands of years had this scene repeated? The goldens made a last flight and the falcon appeared out of nowhere and flew at one threateningly, then slipped out of sight. The goldens headed for their chimney roost. Good night.

Early the next morning, the sun barely up, the bold little falcon was again harassing one of the goldens in the chimney. The golden flew off and came back in a few minutes with its mate. As usual, the falcon was no longer around. All day batches of noisy geese showed up. A few sunny days later one of the goldens fetched twigs to the big nest. Magpies walked along the edges of floating river ice picking up something. I went onto the island to see what they were eating but saw only a hatch of tiny black midges. Could the big, burly magpies be bothered with such minute prey? Why not, if grizzly bears grow fat on August moths? Two chickadees came to the woodpecker picnic that had failed to attract any woodpeckers. Woodpeckers preferred the side of the house or tree trunks. Geese and fast-flying ducks were arriving. It was a good flying day, and two bald eagles, two goldens and three ravens looped around the cliff. The usual crowd of grey-crowned rosy-finches gobbled seed.

Chickadees were rare at Bird Cloud. In Centennial dozens of mountain chickadees came to the feeder on the lee side of the house every day, but I almost never saw them at Bird Cloud. Of course Centennial was close to the forest and Bird Cloud was surrounded by open grazing land. The prevailing weather at Bird Cloud had, as its basic ingredient, a "whistling mane" of wind from the northwest. It built concrete snow-drifts in winter, in summer desiccated plants, hurled sand and gravel and dried clothes in ten minutes. The eagles, falcons and pelicans loved windy days and threw themselves into the sky, catching updrafts that took them to dizzying heights.

Why was it so windy at Bird Cloud? Elevation is a potent factor, so with the top of the cliff checking in at a little more than seven thousand feet above sea level the wind was almost never flat calm, and often like a collapsing mountain of air. We felt the Coriolis effect of the earth's turning. The cliff itself directed the wind along its stony plane face as boaters com-ing down the river knew only too well. I wondered if this was Bernoulli's principle, an increase in wind speed as the air is squeezed between the cliff and the tropopause, the atmospheric boundary between the troposphere and the stratosphere five to ten miles overhead. The nearby mountain ranges of the Sierra Madre and Medicine Bow produce large amplitude gravity waves, wind shear and turbulence. And because vast tracts of land to the west were heavily grazed cow pastures unbroken by trees or shrubs, the wind could rush east unimpeded. And this, I found, rereading Aldo Leopold's *Sand County Almanac,* was deadly for chickadees. "I know several wind-swept wood-lots that are chickless all winter, but are freely used at all other seasons. They are wind-swept because cows have browsed out the undergrowth. To the steam-heated banker who mortgages the farmer who needs more cows who need more pasture, wind is a minor nuisance. . . . To the chickadee, winter wind is the boundary of the habitable world." He adds the true note that "books on nature seldom mention wind; they are written behind stoves."[8]

It was wind-produced snowdrifts on the county road that prevented me from living at Bird Cloud in winter. Yet I could appreciate the raptors' elation when they rose to mad, tilting heights. And the wind is a giver of health and life, cleansing fetid pollution from the atmosphere and transporting count-less seeds to new locations. Two billion years in the past blue-green algae and bacteria had pumped enough oxygen into the atmosphere to make the early ozone layer and shield life-forms from the savage ultraviolet sunlight. The ancient Ordovician wind carried the first land plant spores to barren and empty places, starting the fantastic unfolding of diversity in plant forms, leading to the first flowering plants roughly 140 mil-lion years ago and so on to more than 400,000 species today.

Fresh snow fell overnight and the rosy-finches had learned something from the chickadees. Now they were all fighting over the woodpecker picnic mix as rich suet held the seeds together. I wondered if something was dead at the west end top of the cliff. The goldens were up there, rising and falling, and the balds were there as well. I remembered several years earlier in Centennial when a deer got into our small herb garden, pan-icked by something, tried to squeeze through a six-inch space between fence slats and its broad chest got wedged in, the ani-mal unable to escape. Whatever had frightened it tore out its heart, leaving the body still jammed in the fence. We dragged the carcass down into the willows. A pair of goldens found it within hours and in three days had eaten the entire deer. Now I hoped that whatever attracted the eagles was not one of the elk. I had not seen either for about a week. A little later one of the balds was back in its fishing tree and half a dozen whistler ducks flew over the house with one of the goldens right above them, maybe trying for a feathered jackpot.

As March came in the river deepened and widened. I could just hear the gurgling water from the house. A hawk that fit the description of a juvenile light-morph broad-winged hawk sat for an hour on the most northeasterly branch of the most easterly tree on the island. The head and bib were a dark, rufous brown, the underside pale. Chickadees, grey-crowned rosy-finches, ravens, bald eagles, goldeneyes and a few red-winged blackbirds, a pair of blue-winged teal and a solitary rough-legged hawk were livening up the wind. A few days later ducks and geese were everywhere. And, as I knew they would, the red-winged blackbirds took over the bird feeder. Their main meeting place was the willow thicket on the west end of the island, where hundreds jammed into the same clump, sang and sang and flashed their epaulets, then all flew away only to return and sing and flash again. The prairie falcon cruised back and forth in front of the cliff, its color so like that of the pale rock it was virtually invisible. A marmot showed up from somewhere—the remaining pile of lumber—and took up a station beneath the bird feeder, happy with the spilled seed that the red-wings dropped. Walking down at the east end of the property in a light rain I saw an unusually large marmot on the top of the cliff, peering down. A few hundred yards east I caught a glimpse of a burly coyote as it ducked out of sight. Both were oversize. With hindsight I thought the "marmot" really had been a mountain lion cub and the large "coyote" probably its mother, as I saw both cats at close range later in the spring.

One lovely warm afternoon the goldens were sunning themselves on the cliff top above their nest site. They flew outward, wheeled and returned to a projecting rock they favored. When they flew their shadows also flew along the cliff and it was not easy to sort out the birds from their shadows. The larger golden sat on the rock while the smaller, darker eagle did some fancy wing work, then glided down to its lover, presented it with something small, then mounted her. I had never seen a pair of eagles mate before.

Every day the place showed remarkable changes. The dull mud was inescapable. A few pale green rushes sprouted at the end of the island. The river grew larger and faster. One of the elk reappeared after a two-week absence. It, or they, may have been feeding on the back slope which could not be seen from the house. In midmonth a little burst of warm days cleared most of the ice out of the river. Falcons, ducks, geese, hawks and eagles sped in all directions, coming and going. I counted twenty mountain bluebirds and knew there was a housing shortage. But the ravens, harassed mercilessly by the prairie falcons, abandoned their old nest site. I was left with only the memory of the previous year when four young ravens teetered, flapped, and finally pushed off from the home nest late one afternoon to try their wings.

It had been Memorial Day weekend with friends and relatives and one of the season's first thunderstorms was moving in. The young ravens fluttered and hopped, clung and dropped, flew short distances, always close to the cliff face with its thousand crannies. We watched them with pleasure, but their hopping and unpracticed flying also attracted the attention of every other bird in the vicinity. The bald eagles, red-tailed hawks, the falcon circled or chose high perches suitable for diving attacks. The great horned owls hooted from the island. The storm came on inexorably, dropping first a few splattering drops, then sheets of cold rain that drowned our campfire. I was sure the young ravens were done for. They could not seem to get back to the nest ledge and huddled on narrow shelves or exposed knobs of rock. With sadness we went inside, dreading what the morning would bring. Would any of them survive the waiting predators? Would the storm batter them?

The dawn showed off one of those fragrant, polished days so rare in Wyoming, windless and fresh-washed. We all rushed to the cliff with binoculars wondering if any of the young birds had survived. "I see one!" someone called and then another came into the sunlight from its hiding hole, rather damp and bedraggled. The last two joined them from some cranny and there they all were, preening in the sun, smart and sassy and very much alive. They spent the day practicing evasive flying and I didn't worry about them any longer. But now that was only a memory. In 2007, thanks to the prairie falcons, there would be no young ravens.

An early morning walk on the island brought me face-to-face with a great horned owl two feet away in a willow thicket. So strange. The left eye was brilliant yellow, the right one a rusty brown, very likely from an injury. It fled into a cottonwood and stayed there all day. Now migrating birds flew over constantly, following the river. One afternoon there were six golden eagles on their way to somewhere else but unable to resist playing in the air currents above the cliff. Mallards, mergansers and dippers arrived, then black scoters, a pair of northern flickers, a northern harrier and a single western meadowlark. I found identifying ducks rather difficult because of their various color stages and fast movements. They are also very skittish and high-flying. The river, fed by rapid snowmelt, continued to rise and on the nineteenth of March it was high enough to swing Uphill Bob's bridge onto the island shore, cutting it off from the mainland. The warm days continued, worrisome because everything was drought dry. A forecast for rain brought nothing. When it finally did fall it made the roads into an icy, slippery mush.

One of the Canada geese, no doubt thinking itself clever, built a nest high up on the east end of the cliff, not far from the peregrine falcon nest. I wondered if this was the same foolish goose that had built a nest in the top of a tall tree and open to the sky the year before between the golden eagle nest and the prairie falcons. She and her mate lost all their chicks to predators and had to try again, this time with a nest on the ground beneath the tree and the male standing guard.

In late March a winter storm moved in for a day and a night. Despite the snow and wind a flock of horned larks gleaned seed among the sage and rabbitbrush. The prairie falcon roared down out of nowhere and the larks exploded into fleeing rockets. Other carnivorous birds, especially the bluebirds, sat dejectedly on the fences waiting for spring. When the storm sailed away it left a foot of fresh snow. At the cold sunrise there was a heavy fog over the river which expanded and blotted out the sun. Beneath the snow the ground was wet, half-frozen mud. Just to have someplace to walk I drove the truck back and forth in the driveway, flattening the snow. It seemed to me that the house site was a combination gravel pit, mud slide, snow bowl and wind tunnel.

The snow turned the black metal ravens on the gateposts into magpies. About fifty horned larks were huddled in the sparse shelter of sagebrush plants and crouched in clusters in the driveway. Horned larks, wrote Charles H. Trost in Sibley's *Behavior,* need open ground. They like overgrazed pasture which no doubt makes Wyoming attractive to them.[9] Their hind claws are very long. And like other larks they give fine aerial displays as both sexual attractants and territorial claims. But there were no aerial displays after the storm. A few red-backed dark-eyed juncos showed up, their feathers extravagantly fluffed out against the cold. A few purple finches and mountain chickadees joined them. The red-winged blackbirds divided up, the males at the feeders eating seeds, the females at the woodpecker picnic getting the suet as well as the seeds—building up strength for egg laying? I could not tell if the golden eagle was on its nest. The rim of the nest was white with snow.

April came in windy and warm. On a walk to the east end I found a dead osprey on the ground, its grey feet curled in an empty grasp. There was no way to tell what had brought it to its death. There were so many jealous and territorial birds around—within half a mile two pairs of goldens, red-tailed hawks, one pair of peregrine falcons, and a little farther west the raven family and the fierce prairie falcons—that any one of them might have seen the osprey as an interloper. Spring is the time for death. A calf carcass washed up on the island to the delight of the magpies and perhaps the eagles.

I was not sure of the timing of the bald eagles' family life. They had started fixing up their huge nest, a task that can go on for several months, in December. It looked to be more than six feet across. But I suspected there were young in the nest the first week in April, mostly because I saw one of the bald eagles vigorously chasing a red-tailed hawk nearby. The hawk had been patrolling the western section of cliff for several days

9. Charles H. Trost in David Allen Sibley, *The Sibley Guide to Bird Life and Behavior* (New York: Knopf, 2001), 418.

past. That would put the eagles' egg laying in the last week of February or the first week of March. The female lays two or three eggs over a period of about a week. Both eagles take turns brooding the eggs though the females do more of this duty than the males, both have brood patches on their bellies, bare, hot skin that rests directly on the eggs. On a warm, sunny day both parents can take a little break. Whoever is not on the eggs rustles food. Incubation takes thirty-five days, more or less. Once the young eagles have hatched, exhausting work begins. If the weather is still cold one of the parents stays with the babies and keeps them warm. When the spring sun beats down hot and fierce the parent eagles transform themselves into wide-wing umbrella shades. In the early days the male was kept busy finding and bringing food to the nest, four to eight times a day. After the first few weeks the female hunted as well, and in the late stages of nestling rearing the mother did most of the hunting. (I assumed the larger bird was the female, according to the ornithological books.)

The eagles fought and chased red-tailed hawks away from the nest day after day. I was sure there were fledglings in the nest. But I was gone for two weeks and missed all the action. When I got back the third week in April the American white pelicans had arrived, big knobs on their beaks showing it was breeding time in their world. The pelicans were fabulous fliers and on windy days put on astonishing exhibitions of soaring and diving. One of the sad things about Wyoming was the ignorant fishermen who shot pelicans because they believed the birds would eat all the fish, leaving nothing for them. That first spring at Bird Cloud I was appalled by all the big, fluffy white carcasses that floated down the river. Fortunately there were none in subsequent years.

When I returned from a trip to Ireland in the middle of May, the air was stitched with hundreds and hundreds of swallows. Several persistent rough-winged swallows, remembering the kindness of the James Gang the summer before, tried to build nests in the house eaves. I found a dead pelican at the end of the island, the head completely gone, no other sign of injury. Gerald remarked that it was the habit of cats to eat the head first. I did not think the mountain lion would bother with a pelican or, if it did, restrict its dinner to the head. But a well-placed shot with a large-caliber rifle, or a shotgun could have blown the head off. To reduce the number of porcupine dens I started piling up dead wood and fallen branches on the island, planning to have a bonfire on a rainy day. There was plenty of undisturbed room for them on the other side of the river. A tiny, dark house wren had found the wren-size birdhouse on the island and was moving in, carrying twigs not much larger than toothpicks and wisps of dead grass.

It was a big thrill when I saw a white-faced ibis near the front gate where there was irrigation overflow. The ibis stayed around for weeks. A few days after this sighting I was sitting near the river and saw two herons fly to the bald eagles' favorite fishing tree. They were too small to be great blue herons, and did not really look like little blues. A few minutes with the heron book cleared up the mystery; they were tricolored herons, the first I had ever seen.[10] By the end of the month American goldfinches were shooting around like tossed gold pieces despite another cold spell.

Suddenly it was mid-June and noxious weeds—leafy spurge, cheatgrass, hoary cress, Canada thistle—grew everywhere. Nests were full of young birds and the predator birds, who had

---

10. James Hancock, *Herons of North America: Their World in Focus* (San Diego, London: Academic Press, 2000), 43–45.

hatched their young earlier, had rich pickings. Even a raiding great blue heron flew over pursued by smaller birds. My Game and Fish friends Ron and Andrea came to float the river. Andrea was doing an eagle count and they were clearly abundant in this river corridor. As we approached the east end of Bird Cloud's cliff Andrea spied a parent prairie falcon and four young, all lined up silent and quiet, rather resembling a quintet of Egyptian mummies, on a ledge above our heads. I hadn't dared go near the fence across from the big nest for fear of forcing the goldens to abandon, but I could see now that they had two big chicks in the nest. And this month was marked by the appearance of an insect I had never seen before—*Eremobates pallipes,* a.k.a. wind scorpion, a resident of deserts and the Great Basin. It was straw-colored, about three-fourths of an inch long and very much resembled a scorpion although it is not poisonous. It will bite if disturbed. It feeds on small insects, so I caught this one and put it outside hoping it could catch mosquitoes. More likely it made a snack for the myriad of hungry birds rushing around outside.

I came back from a wonderful week in Capri in time for a hot, dusty Fourth of July, rather a red-letter day for many young birds taking their first flights. I walked down the road to the east end, pleased not to be cursed by the parent goldens. One of their big dark chicks had found a narrow shelf with an overhanging ceiling not far from the nest and there it sat, harassed by—who else?—the prairie falcon. But even young goldens are tough and fierce and the falcon departed. When I got back from my walk I found some bird had dropped the corpse of a large nestling on the deck, white downy feathers, wings not fully fledged, the head gone. I thought it might have been the chick of a great blue heron or sandhill crane.

The drought was bad, very hot and dry day after day and no

rain for a long time. The grass cracked and broke when stepped on and it was too hot to sleep at night. Wind scorpion weather. The James Gang was still not finished with the siding and the weeks dragged on. But during the final night of the month it rained, easing the terrible heat buildup and reviving the land. I opened the front door for the damp, delicious air and to hear the eagles crying on the river side and the sandhill cranes in the bull pasture. The kingfisher, a bird we don't see very often, sat briefly in the bald eagles' fishing tree, the cause, no doubt, of all the eagle screeches. The rain triggered an explosion of insects, especially midges which rose in clouds above the willows on the island and the river. In the evening twilight countless hundreds of swallows flew through them at high speed with their mouths open, resembling predator fish slicing into a knot of terrified herring.

The respite was brief. A hard, hot wind dried out the lettuces in the garden, tearing petals off any flowers not made of steel. But the young eagles, both bald and golden, loved this heated air. They and their parents were all soaring and zooming, trick-flying, mounting high and then rolling down the air currents. At one point I could see seven eagles flying above the cliff at various altitudes, some so high they resembled broken paper clips.

The wind died away and one evening a friend came to dinner. We sat outside enjoying the gathering dusk. A lone goose flew downriver, honking. The silence of late summer descended. We sat saying nothing, hearing nothing. Then there was a loud *HSSSSHHHH!* sound as a goose landed in shallow water. A full moon rose, transforming a jet contrail into a comet, and the river glimmered through the trees. It was a lovely evening until we noticed something ridiculous that made us laugh. The James Gang had installed underground water sprinklers and dotted around in the grass were small valve covers, about four inches across, each with a nickel-size hole in the top. As my friend and I sat in the moonlight we watched one little head after another pop out of the holes in the valve covers—mice! A wee head would show, a mouse would emerge as if it were a sewer worker coming up through a manhole, and the rodent would scamper to the edge of the deck and dive under, followed by another and another. We counted ten mice coming out from one valve cover. The James Gang was not amused to hear this and stopped up the holes in the covers with wine corks.

By the tenth of August I could see a nervous change in the avian population. Flocks of birds seemed to be forming, bunching up. Two ravens came to the cliff and flew around their ledge nest site of yesteryear. Were they the old residents checking out their once-happy home? I thought so, because one of them had a white spot on its cheek which I remembered had distinguished one of the earlier residents. When I first noticed it I thought of Ernest Thomson Seton's Silverspot, a crow with a similar mark. And one of the crows that foraged in the tidal pools in front of our Newfoundland house also had a white spot on its left cheek. So perhaps such marks are common among crows and ravens. If these were the old residents they must have been disappointed as the cliff was alive with falcons and eagles and red-tailed hawks. It was now a predator cliff. Of course ravens are no mean opportunists themselves, and the only reason to think of them as victims of the prairie falcon was my fondness for corvids.

A few mornings later a bird with an ineffably beautiful song woke me. I had no idea what it was and it was not visible from the high bedroom windows. I tried to identify it from bird-song CDs without success. It was the harbinger of a nasty little frost, a complete surprise, that killed the tops of my tomato plants and beans, scorched the zucchini and cucumbers. I didn't realize it but the surprise mid-August frost would be an annual event at Bird Cloud, striking just when the garden was approaching high ripeness.

At the end of the month the James Gang set off for their annual camping and prospecting trip on Mount Antero in Colorado. Before they left Dave and Deryl planted thirty new shrubs. As soon as they were out of sight a robin began an inspection tour on foot. It walked up to and around every new plant and stone, closely examining each. The entire inspection took about fifteen minutes for the shrubs at the back of the house. Of course I don't know, but I suspect that robin was memorizing the good and bad qualities of each of those plants.

On the first of September, while making coffee in the kitchen I glanced up at the cliff and saw the big tawny-red mountain lion walking along the top. It descended to an area of outcrop above and to the right of two huge square stones balanced almost on the edge. It was impossible to see this area from the top. Three weeks later, just before dark, I glassed the cliff and the colluvium piles below and noticed a large round rock on the debris cone that I couldn't remember seeing before. The telescope revealed it as a dead deer that had apparently fallen from the top of the cliff. Falling off a cliff was not something even the most addlepated deer would do. I surmised the lion had chased the panicked deer over the edge, and until dark I kept peering through the telescope, looking for the lion to claim its kill. But the lion did not come.

The next morning two ravens were on the carcass but unable to break through the hide. As I made coffee I noticed that the ravens were gone, replaced by thirty magpies and two coyotes. It took the coyotes half an hour to break through the hide. The bald eagles perched nearby, waiting their chance, and several ravens also waited. One of the coyotes departed. There was no sign of the lion. By midmorning the remaining coyote, bloody-muzzled and gorged, waddled away reluctantly. The magpies moved in. The most cautious diners were the eagles and ravens who waited until after eleven for a turn at the deer. The first coyote returned with two friends and all three began to tug the carcass toward the edge of the colluvium pile, a drop-off of about ten feet. By afternoon the carcass was no longer in sight, now fallen into the brush below where perhaps the lions would claim it. The renegade thought now occurred to me that perhaps the neighbor's cow that had fallen off the cliff the year before had been chased to its death by the lion.

In the first days of September the prairie falcons left, and the next week the ravens were back. I heard a heavy croaking when I went to the garage, so close it sounded in the garage. The bird was likely perched on the owl roost Gerald had put at the east end of the house. (Some visitors complain that owls keep them awake at night.) Were the ravens just checking things out? Had they come to spend the winter?

On the eighteenth the first bird to fall by flying into a window of this house did so at dusk. It was a lesser goldfinch. I left it on the deck and in the morning it was gone—I hope because it revived. Many birds knock themselves out and then come back from apparent death rather groggy and confused, but alive. The big, handsome northern flicker is an aggressive bird that often hurls itself at its reflection, falls like a stone, lies on its back with its feet curled up for a while, opens one eye, gets shakily up and staggers through the air to a nearby branch where it spends an hour or two thinking black thoughts—and then flies into the window again.

The days were shortening and the light on the cliff was changing in hue. At sunset the cliff glowed in the amazing color of the flesh of the Hubbard squash, a deep yellow-orange. I began to think about the winter, knowing I couldn't stay at Bird Cloud after the serious snow started. Yet I planned to stay as long as I could.

Once more we were unwilling hosts to a mess of cows, these from upriver. They trampled and ruined Deryl's freshly seeded lawn. Two years later the imprints of their hooves were still visible. We got a fencer to put an emergency hot-wire around the island which was the cows' favorite place, and arranged with the new fencer to take on the job of enclosing the north shore along the river and the island with buck fence. Cows will try to push through a wire fence or even leap over it—these big animals can jump rather well when they want—and have more respect for a sturdy wooden buck fence.

By the twenty-seventh most of the migratory birds were gone. I remembered an earlier September when some friends and I had camped at the top of Green Mountain where we could look down at the Red Desert and make out the old stage-coach road and a few bunches of wild horses. We hiked around, noticed quite a few hawks, and by midmorning realized that the hawk migration was in full spate. Hundreds of hawks flew over us that day, swiftly, seriously intent on getting away. Also intent, not on getting away, but on filling up great pantries with pine seeds, were grey jays. They would cram seed after seed into their pouches and then take them to their secret caches. One smart grey jay, trying to pack in more than his crop could hold, hopped (heavily) to a little pool of water in the top of a boulder, took a few sips to wet down the seeds, and resumed gathering.

By mid-October most of the birds had gone south. The meadowlarks were the last to leave. The golden eagles were somewhere else, though probably in the area. The bald eagles were involved in a major undertaking—the building of a new nest in a cottonwood closer to the river and closer to our house. One eagle flew in with a double-talon bunch of cut hay, likely swiped from TA hay bales. This new nest, unlike the old one, was highly visible. I worried about people who floated the river in summer. Not so many years ago local ranchers killed eagles on sight, even fish-eating bald eagles. What were the birds thinking? Did they plan to fish from the nest? Of course, this eagle pair has showed they are more interested in river traffic and what we are doing around the house than in privacy and isolation. As with humans, in the bird world it takes all kinds. It should be excellent eagle watching for us, even when the leaves are out. For weeks they hauled materials in, much like an avian James Gang, mostly sticks and a dangerous length of orange binder twine that could tangle young birds tramping around in the nest. They took breaks from the construction and went fishing at the east end of the cliff, something they would not do when the goldens were in residence. But were the goldens really gone? There were a few days of rain and wet snow that made the county road a slithery mass of greasy mud.

On the first of November I walked along the river fence line in the evening and as I came abreast of the big nest the scolding *"Get away, fool!"* call came from the cliff. The goldens were in their bedroom niche.

Colder and colder the days, clear and windless, the kind of day I have loved since my New England childhood. The rough-legged hawk, a visiting stranger in these parts, came hunting over the fields. The bald eagles did something unusual—they chased it furiously, asserting their territorial rights. The hawk fled. The new nest looked large and commodious. The day after Thanksgiving a Clark's nutcracker appeared briefly on one of Deryl's shrubs, but it had dark markings on its face like a small black mask, and looked a little like a grey jay though the body and wings were utterly Clark's. I saw it for only a few seconds before it sprang away, but it seemed that very often I saw birds that are subtly at variance with Sibley's illustrations.

Near the end of the month a little warm wind pushed in a bank of cloud. A northern harrier coursed over the bull pasture, just barely skimming the grass, floating on and on in lowest gear, then landing in the distant grass, hidden from me. It rose again, higher, using the wind. One morning one of the bald eagles brought a hefty stick to the new nest. It was long and awkward, and to get it in place the bird had to circle behind the nest and trample it in from the back with the help of its mate. It was a really big nest. A few hours later a bold raven came and sat on the west branch of the bald eagles' fishing tree, about twenty feet away from the male eagle. They both seemed uneasy. The raven pretended unconcern and stretched his wings. The eagle shifted from one foot to the other as if muttering "What is this clown doing in my tree?" The big female eagle came in for a landing and sat beside her mate, and as she put down her landing gear the raven took off.

In the afternoon the wind strengthened after four days of calm and the goldens enjoyed it, rising into the empyrean until they seemed to dissolve in blue. It was like one of the Arabian Nights tales in reverse, the tale where someone fleeing looked back and saw something the size of a grain of sand pursuing, and a little later looked again and saw something the size of a lentil. Later still the pursuer resembled a beetle, then a rabbit and finally a slavering, demonic form on a maddened camel. But to my eyes the goldens shrank first to robin size, then to wrens, then hummingbirds and finally gnats or motes of dust high in the tremulous ether. Just before grey twilight the northern harrier returned, but strayed into enemy airspace above the cliff, and suddenly there were four ravens chasing and nipping. The extra pair of ravens came from nowhere, like black origami conjured from expert fingers. As darkness swelled up from the east a full moon rose and illuminated great sheets of thin cloud like wadded fabric drawn across its pock-marked white face.

What a frisson! Turning the pages of a large book on wild-life conservation in Wyoming I came across a full-page photograph of our cliff across from the big hole where the young eagles stood on a sandbar and watched for little fish. The photograph was taken in the late nineteenth century and nothing had changed. Nothing. It looks exactly the same—as many places in Wyoming do. A few years ago Mary Meagher and Douglas B. Houston assembled a number of photographs of Yellowstone taken in the nineteenth century, then found the long-gone photographer's vantage points and took new photographs to compare with the old.[11] Changes, when visible, were subtle. In many cases the same trees—usually much taller and wider, but sometimes fallen—were still there. Almost all of the photographs were close matches with the present day.

November fell through the floor and December began with the tingling, fresh scent of snow. Seven or eight inches fell. I had hoped this month would be snow-free, but it looked like that hope was dashed. Night after night I had bad sinus headaches, an allergic reaction to something—but what?—I had eaten. The bald eagles kept on fluffing up their new nest. The TA cows in the west pasture had a certain way of eating. They grasped a bunch of grass and with a sharp jerk pulled it sideways. I supposed that at this time of year it broke off rather

---

11. Mary Meagher and Douglas B. Houston, *Yellowstone and the Biology of Time: Photographs Across a Century* (Norman: University of Oklahoma Press, 1998).

smartly. The bald eagles liked to collect nest materials early in the morning. Just after first light I saw one swoop down on the cows, snatch up a clump of broken-off grass, practically from the mouth of the cow, and carry it to the nest. The early bird gets the mattress stuffing.

I could not leave Bird Cloud until I finished the edit of the Red Desert book, but the snow and wind kept coming. There was little time for watching birds, and getting the mail or supplies was chancy. Usually I could put the old Land Cruiser in low and smash through the drifts, but in places the wind had packed the snow into unsmashable drifts and I got well and truly stuck on the county road. I tried to barrel through a five-foot drift that looked fluffy, small in comparison to the big piles that would come later in the winter, and ended up high-centered on a solid pedestal of snow, all four wheels off the ground. Once again the James Gang saved the day with shovels, cursing and a strong tow band. It snowed again just before Christmas, deep and beautiful snow that lay quiet in a rare calm. The hero sun came out for a quarter hour, then fell as though wounded. Eagles and goldeneyes were the only birds around. At dusk I skied down to the Jack Creek bridge. Mist rose from the river and the cliff seemed to be melting, the top floating on quivering froth.

The next morning was very cold, trees and shrubs frosted with the last night's mist. In the pre-sunrise light they took on delicate pink and violet hues. The cliff showed pinkish beige as if wearing a peach-skin cloak. In the pastures the black cows crowded around the haystacks, their coats as frosted as the willow twigs. The sun cleared the edge of the world and the wind shot forward, kicking the peachy rose snow hills into glittering explosions. Gerald came and broke a trail through the snow so I could get out, but I didn't have anywhere to go. Yet.

The next day was very cold, only 10°F at noon. It snowed all morning and Gerald came again, keeping the lane open by bashing through. The eagles sat calm and in their tree watching for fish below in a narrow strip of open water. The day ended with a sense of urgency. How long could Gerald keep the lane open? How long could I stay?

I made it down to the last days of December. It was 15°F below zero and the snow squealed when I walked on it. Late in the morning I saw the pair of golden eagles flying high over the cliff, playing in the frigid air. It began snowing again and I decided I would try to get out the next day. The lane was half-choked with snow and even Gerald couldn't keep it clear much longer. If I didn't go the next day I knew I could be isolated for a long time, jailed at the end of the impassable road. I packed the old Land Cruiser and fled to New Mexico.

So ended the first and only full year I was to spend at Bird Cloud. I returned in March and for several more years came in early spring and stayed until the road-choking snow drove me out, but I had to face the fact that no matter how much I loved the place it was not, and never could be, the final home of which I had dreamed.

Postscript

The ruined eagle nest

In April 2010 I returned to Bird Cloud to catch up on the lives of the avian population of the cliff. If you watch birds you soon realize how dangerous are their lives. Wyoming winter is a hard time for even these hardy creatures, but the snares and instruments of humans are more deadly than weather, and only rarely do you learn what has happened. There were no golden eagles at the big nest and no way to know why.

At the bald eagle nest—almost doubled in size—I could not see the head of an eagle sitting on eggs, although one or the other should have been there. One of the bald eagles sat on their favorite fishing tree and flew over when I first came out of the house, as curious as ever. But as the days passed I only saw that one eagle, never two. The nest looked empty. Then the single eagle was gone.

Gerald fixed the Bush Hog mower which had broken down last fall and decided to finish mowing the margin of the entry lane. He discovered the wing and corpse remains of an eagle on the TA side of the fence. It was under Bird Cloud's new safer-design power line put up in 2004 by the local electric coop. Gerald thought it might be a golden eagle, but when I looked at what was left, there were so many shining white neck feathers caught in the tough grass that I knew it had to be one of the bald eagles. We do not know exactly what killed it.

Eagles waste no time on tears. The day after the lone eagle disappeared I saw in the sky far to the west two tiny bird shapes soaring, diving, touching, clasping talons and tumbling. I knew immediately that the lone eagle had found a handsome widow or a young unmated eagle. Just before dark the two flew to the cliff and it was obvious that the lone eagle was showing his domain to the new bride. Suddenly the new eagle took off, heading west, and the lone eagle pursued her. I assumed she didn't like the place. But the next morning there were two eagles in the tree above the river. It was too late in the season to raise a family, the common wildlife situation of hope deferred.

ABOUT THE AUTHOR

Annie Proulx is the author of *The Shipping News* and three other novels, *That Old Ace in the Hole, Postcards,* and *Accordion Crimes,* and the story collections *Heart Songs, Close Range, Bad Dirt,* and *Fine Just the Way It Is*. Her story "Brokeback Mountain," which originally appeared in *The New Yorker,* was made into an Academy Award–winning film. She has won the Pulitzer Prize, a National Book Award, the *Irish Times* International Fiction Prize, and the PEN/Faulkner Award, and was recently inducted into the American Academy of Arts and Letters. She lives in Wyoming and New Mexico.